The WAITING ROOM BOOK

The WAITING ROOM BOOK

Your Friend to Help You and Your
Loved Ones through the Diagnosis

Joanna Chanis

Printed in the United States of America
First Printing, 2020

ISBN-13: 978-1-949001-98-3 print edition
ISBN-13: 978-1-949001-99-0 ebook edition

An imprint of:

Waterside Productions
2055 Oxford Ave
Cardiff, CA 92007
www.waterside.com
www.DreamSculpt.com

"Joanna is truly a gift. In this book, she shows her vulnerability in such a courageous way to help others on their healing journey. She is the friend that you need who is completely honest and, at times, funny too. Joanna will always hold a special place in my heart as she has helped me heal and find my best self, using this same advice she presents in her book. I know many people will find comfort and joy in this book. All is well."

Tonya H., healed from breast cancer

"I finished your ten-week story, feeling blessed. Grateful for sharing it with me. I cried with you, I felt your pain and despair, your fear and rage. I am now feeling stronger, more confident and hopeful through your point of view and your guidance. A lot of women will be fortunate to receive the blessing of this book. Thank you so much, God bless you and answer all your prayers, Love you, my lighthouse from above."

Maro Papoutsa, healed from breast cancer

Dedication:

For Melina and Thalia. Thank you for your love, compassion, courage, and confidence… you light up my life.

Acknowledgments:

Thank you to Vasili for always believing I can do anything. Thank you to my book coach, Jared Rosen, for organizing my book and for guiding me, this book would not have been possible without you. Thank you to my editor, Joyce Walker, it was such a pleasure to work with you. Thank you to Melina Mourmoutis for making my vision for the book cover come to life. Thank you to Thalia Mourmoutis for being the cover model. Thank you to all my Kumbari here and in Greece. Thank you to my friends, old and new. Thank you to my best friend. Thank you to my parents here on Earth and in heaven. Thank you to my family. Thank you to Taylor Wells. Thank you to Apollonia Holzer—a true angel on Earth. Thank you to Dr. Ellis for showing me another way. Thank you to Rachel Rosovsky for your guidance and compassion. Thank you to my neighbor Sue Stahl. Thank you, Sister Barbara Rogers and the community at NCDS. Thank you to my prayer circle. Thank you to my SoulCycle community. Thank you, Fr. Dimitri and the community at the Annunciation Cathedral of New England. Thank you to all my doctors, nurses, and staff at Massachusetts General Hospital. Thank you to all who prayed for me and my family. Thank you, God.

Introduction

The reason I wrote this book was it was exactly what I would have needed after my breast cancer diagnosis but couldn't find. You see, I was caught between the two worlds—the spiritual, holistic side and the medical, scientific side. I found and read many helpful books on both sides, and I am so grateful for all they taught me. But I still found myself somewhere in the middle between the two. I was and still am a very spiritual and faithful person. Still, I wasn't comfortable with surrendering to a completely holistic approach. But I am also a person who was extremely conservative medically, so deciding to have a double mastectomy and whatever ongoing treatment the doctors recommended was a big decision for me.

I knew deep down that no matter how incredible my surgeons and doctors were, and they were all amazing, if I didn't get myself right inside that they wouldn't be able to fully do their jobs. So I set forth on a journey that was a hybrid, combining the two to find a space that felt right for me. During this process, I met a woman who was going through a similar diagnosis just a few weeks behind me. I would share what I had learned with her along the way, and it helped us both get through our diagnosis and heal. I am so fortunate that she has now become a dear friend. One of my silver linings of sure.

I started to write this book when I was six weeks post-surgery. It had started as something different, what I thought people would want to read, a little guarded. Then, a few weeks into writing, my daughter Melina came to me and said, "Mom, I hope your book is honest, because I hear you crying every night in your bathroom." She was right. If I was going to really help people, I needed to be honest. That day I put aside everything holding me back, and I opened my heart and wrote. Thank you for reading.

Table of Contents:

Chapter One: The Shocking Call. 1

Chapter Two: Heaven in Harlem 41

Chapter Three: The Jo Inside 53

Chapter Four: The Love Shift 67

Chapter Five: The Renewal of Faith. 89

Chapter Six: Purgatory in Purgatory 101

Chapter Seven: The Next Chapter 133

About the Author 141

Chapter One: The Shocking Call

Strong Bonds

It was past six o'clock on a Thursday night, and I figured it must be an annoying telemarketer, but when I saw the number, my heart stopped. It was my doctor, and I could immediately tell by the sound of his voice that the news wasn't what we had hoped. Then the sentence that I feared for the past 15 years came: "Joanna, the biopsy results tested positive and you have breast cancer." Time stood still. I could hear his words, but I could not comprehend anything that he was saying, my mind was fixated on time. My two teenage daughters were going to walk in at any moment, and I was in such a state of shock I knew I wasn't ready to face them.

My instinct took over and I went into "logistical mode," although everything was in slow motion except for my heart, which was beating as fast as my mind was racing. Although I was home, I became disoriented and couldn't recognize where I was. I went into my bedroom and called my husband, who was still at work, to tell him the shocking news. We made a very quick plan to meet at the restaurant across the street once he settled the girls after dinner. I called my best friend, Joy, who is a mother of five children. She dropped what she was doing and came to meet me. We are very close and have been friends for 15 years. She knew everything about my life situation and, like in so many previous moments in my life, was right there with her calm, comforting way to hold my hand and wipe my tears. I was numb.

My husband, who was in his own personal state of shock, joined us and we sat for hours talking. I could see that they were scared. The people in my life I could count on no matter what. They knew me at times better than I knew myself. They could see right through me in any situation and guide me. That night was no different. I was so grateful to my friend so many times before in my life, but never more than at that moment. My husband and I were in the middle of a very challenging time in our marriage; we had even talked that summer about separating. It was nice to have her support for the both of us; we were both so broken we couldn't see beyond our fear. I felt like I was in a movie watching myself. That night, my life had completely changed. I was a different woman. Over the next ten weeks, I went through a metamorphosis, a complete transformation.

Joy and I had met in the lobby of our gym many years ago because I was in tears after a sleepless night with my new baby girl who had colic. She walked up to me like an angel and asked if I was okay, to which I replied, "No, I am not okay. My baby has colic and I haven't slept for a month." She looked at me with her deep, beautiful blue eyes, took my hand, and told me that she had just been through months of colic with her baby boy and that it was over. She assured me it would get better and that everything would be okay. I believed her. She had this very trusting kind face, and you could see that she was real and so genuine. My instinct was right; she was all those things and more.

Throughout the years since, we have had so many good times, endless hours of laughter, and lots of fun with our husbands and children who are also friends. We have gone through so many happy life moments: births of children (in her case three more!), birthday celebrations, graduations, First Communions, confirmations, holidays, vacations, and, of course, Super Bowl parties. So many wonderful memories filled with joyful laughter and champagne.

She was always the first one I would call, the voice of calm and reason. When things got difficult, or there was a "situation," as we would refer to anything that was causing us stress, we would talk to each other and listen and come up with solutions to the problem at hand. She would always know what to say to make me feel better, or just listen when there was nothing to say. This time was no different. In fact, she and my husband were the only two people who knew how anxious I was about having mammograms. Two years earlier, when the doctor had found another lump (that ended up benign) in my right breast, it was she who came to the biopsy with me and held my trembling feet so that the doctor could perform the procedure. She knew how terrified I was of this and that this is the diagnosis I feared for so long. So, when I called her and told her the results, she dropped everything and quickly ran to my side. When I walked into the restaurant across the street from my apartment where we had met countless times over the years, I could see in her face that she was scared. We sat holding hands and I was so shocked I couldn't even cry.

We waited for my husband to join us once he had gotten the girls settled. My husband and I agreed that he would wait for the girls to come home from their second day of school and have dinner with them and then come meet us. We didn't want the girls to know anything until we had time to process everything first. He would tell the girls that I had gone over to meet Joy, and that I would wait until it was late and then come home so I wouldn't have to face them. That was the plan, and it worked, although they later told me that they had an idea that something was going on, but they weren't sure what.

That summer had been an extremely hard time for our marriage. We were fighting daily and were in a very bad place. Although we had tried to put up a good front for the girls when we were together over the weekends, they could tell that we were not in a good place. In the summer, the girls and I move to our summer house in Rhode Island, and my husband came on the weekends from the city. It was a very disconnected summer for us as a couple. Our family unit was strong, but the girls were now teenagers, and it's as if there was a spotlight on the huge gaps in our marriage all of a sudden. I wasn't happy and I thought about leaving. We were just not aligned and hadn't been for many years. I believed in marriage and staying together, but I also knew that I could no longer be the one to hold the whole family together. We both brought our own issues into our marriage from our past; his were left unresolved, and that was a big part of our stress. I had grown frustrated, and that had manifested into anger and rage and he had completely shut down. We are complete personality opposites. In the midst of all of this though, I knew I still loved him. There was something that connected us on a soul level. At moments it would bring me back, and that's why I didn't leave.

Joy and I were sitting in a booth across from each other when my husband came and sat next to me. He is very quiet by nature, the complete opposite of me that way. He is a kind, methodical, and loyal person. He takes his time to speak, but when he does, his words are very well thought out and impactful. He is extremely smart, and in ways, I looked up to him. But on that night, he was completely shut down like he had been for most of the 22 years we were married. He was sitting with his arms crossed over his body. This frustrated me more than ever. I was already so scared and now was more worried than ever if he was going to be able to be there for me at all on an emotional level.

Our marriage had suffered for so long from a lack of intimacy, and I felt emotionally starved. This was not anyone's fault in particular. I think this had been going on for so long that we had been taking turns hurting each other. In fact, it had become our normal. I would blame him, and he would blame me, we would fight about it, and then start all over the next day. That is how it had been for the past three months. I was exhausted, and with everything going on, I was worried if our marriage would be able to survive. I was wondering that if I would survive this diagnosis, would our marriage still be like it had been. This was the predominant thought I had and my major concern. I knew that everything that was no longer working would have to be removed, just like cancer.

I had grown tired of speaking in wishes about what our marriage "would be like one day." I think getting a diagnosis like this puts you on a different clock. What was going on and had been going on forever in our relationship was going to have to be put in a different place for now. I had spent most of my life with my husband trying to please him, trying to be the best I could for our family. Making myself a priority was never on the radar, just like most women. I tried very hard to be the best wife I could, I made a lot of mistakes, but I know I tried my best with my whole heart. This made me sad because I was always so hopeful that things would get better. I knew that if they didn't change now after this diagnosis, then they never would. This was the undertone of even the day I got the call I had cancer: I was still worried about my marriage.

That night I saw clearly that I would have to set up a strong network of family and friends to help get me, my husband, and my daughters through this. I needed to feel love and supported and cared for. I couldn't do it alone.

My husband left to be with the girls, and Joy and I sat for a bit longer. I don't even remember exactly what we talked about. I just found comfort in being with her. At moments like these, you don't know what to do next. At least I didn't. I didn't want to be out, but I also didn't want to be home. I didn't want to talk, but I didn't want to be quiet. It's unlike anything I have ever experienced. She urged me to call my sister when I got home even though it was late and she was traveling for her work, and that felt like the most natural next step. When we walked out of the restaurant on this warm evening, we hugged before she got into her Uber, and she whispered in my ear, "Jo, you are going to be okay. You have to be." One of my greatest gifts in this life is my friendships, especially hers.

Two Sisters

I was scared, I was shaking, I was devastated. My mind was racing, my emotions were overwhelming, and I was just a complete mess. All of my mindful practices went out the window, and I was hysterical. I phoned my sister to share the news, even though our relationship had been nonexistent and very strained for the past seven years. That didn't seem to matter to me anymore, and all I wanted was to talk to her. She was in India on a work trip and I was able to reach her immediately even with the time difference. That was the first sign of how many good things would come from this situation, although I couldn't see it at the moment. I spoke with her, and in that one phone call, I knew we were going to be okay, and that is where my healing journey began. At that moment.

My sister and I had grown up extremely close. In fact, I feel that the day she was born was my first memory of love. I was six years old and had been hoping and praying for a sibling for as long as I could remember. She was everything I imagined and more, a perfectly beautiful little baby girl. Like my own real-life doll. I fell in love with her immediately and never could have imagined that as adults we would go seven years without speaking to each other. I would have been willing to bet my life that was never going to be the case for us. After all, we were inseparable, talking multiple times a day and being very much involved in every aspect of each other's lives. We had been through so much together as children, as teenagers, and well into our adult life.

It was very common for us to talk five times per day; it was like oxygen to me, that instinctual. So when we stopped speaking suddenly, it literally took my breath away. I struggled for years with this. I went through every emotion: anger, resentment, blame, sadness, rage and after many years of our timing just being off and not being able to reconnect, I finally found acceptance in our situation. The timing of this was just a few weeks prior to my diagnosis. Although we had become cordial for the sake of our children, we were still not in a great place. But in August my sister had reached out to me and we met for dinner with our children.

That night, I felt that we were finding our rhythm together again. That this was the beginning of the new version of our relationship. A new chapter for us. I was hopeful, it felt natural, and I embraced it wholeheartedly. I never could have imagined that this was happening after so many years, seemingly out of nowhere, just at the perfect time. God makes no mistakes.

After speaking to my sister and telling her my news, it was very late, so I went to bed. There I lay for hours, wide awake once more; this night was the worst night yet. My mind had completely taken over, coupled with the three glasses of wine I had had since the call from my doctor. I was a hot mess. I had decided that I would wait to tell my daughters until we were all together over the weekend so they could have some time to process. This was the hardest part. I am very close with my girls and we lived in a small space, so hiding this was very difficult. That morning, I sent them off to school, and I know they could feel the sadness I worked so hard to choke back. I was on my way to share my sad news with the person who brought me into the world— my mother.

Hi Mom, I Have Cancer

As I turned the corner onto Boylston Street at 7:30 a.m., which I had done thousands of times over the 15 years of living on my street, I saw a large group of people crossing the street—I would estimate about 200—all wearing pink in honor of raising awareness for breast cancer. I looked up and laughed and said out loud, "Really Dad, you just can't make this shit up." My dad had passed away when I was 16, and I had always had an ongoing dialogue with him ever since. I would always look for signs or could feel him around me, and this was no exception.

Like so many that would be with me helping me, loving me, and supporting me, I also felt my father with me as well. My tone with him at this point was a bit different, not as sweet as it usually was. I was confused; how could he let this happen? Was he not watching me? Did he not realize I had been through so much already? Luckily, I could see that this was exactly what I needed at the perfect time in order for me to truly heal inside. I now understand, and I am more confident than ever that my dad never left me and is with me every day.

I felt numb, time had stopped. Was this happening? I was watching myself go through all these emotions, but everything was slow. As I drove to Worcester that morning, I started to call my friends. I wanted a team of love and support and prayers. This is what felt natural to me. But as the words would come out of my mouth each time, I felt like I was in a Hallmark movie. A movie I didn't want to watch, and even worse, I was the leading lady in the movie.

As a parent myself, I couldn't imagine hearing anything worse than something like this about my child. So even though my relationship with my mother was strained and we had never really gotten along, my heart broke for her and I could see her pain. After telling her and my stepfather and stepbrother, I was back on my way to Boston. Still numb. My mother had remarried a few years after my father had passed away. Her new husband already had two children, and so we quickly became the Greek *Brady Bunch*. The four of us kids had a special bond from the very beginning. Once the parents had started dating and they realized they were going to get married, they took us to a therapist to make sure that we got along, and after speaking with us, the therapist said to our parents, "The kids are fine, but I think the two of you should come back to see me." We still laugh about this today, over 25 years later.

When I pulled off the familiar exit in Worcester, my hometown, I called my parents' restaurant to make sure that they were both there. It was very early in the morning and my stepbrother answered. I asked him for help. Within seconds, I told him that I was about to pull in and had to tell the "rents," as we jokingly refer to them, about my diagnosis. As we hung up the phone, I felt comfort in knowing he had my back and that he was going to help me break the news. My parents' restaurant is small and bright and quiet at this time in the morning. My parents are usually running around very high energy and "yelling," which is really the Greek form of talking to each other.

When I walked in, my mom and stepfather were sitting quietly at the corner table where we have sat hundreds of times throughout the 25 years. They were both calm and sitting quietly, which was one of the first of many miracles to follow.

I didn't overthink or have time to waste, as it was obvious I was there to share some not-so-great news with them. I never liked going back to Worcester in general and went only on holidays or when absolutely necessary. So the fact that I was there so early in the morning, looking like I'd been hit by a truck, probably gave away the fact that I wasn't there to share some great news. I just came out with it. I kept it simple and said the lump that I had biopsied came back positive for cancer and there would be next steps to determine what the plan was going to be. I think I was still in shock because I didn't even cry at that point. It was the first time I told anyone in person. This was different than telling people on the phone. Not easier or harder, just different. You see their reactions and can actually hug, which is nice, but for me at that moment, I was also more aware of my reaction because others were watching. After that experience, I decided to share my news on the phone with people first to give me that buffer.

After I shared my news, a few predictable things happened. The reason I had gone to Worcester to tell my parents in person was that I wanted to avoid having people come by to hang out at my house to talk about this. Also, I hadn't told my girls yet, so it was important for me to keep things as normal as possible. Then my mother declared as I was leaving her restaurant that she would come visit me later, and so it began. My complicated relationship with my mother was front and center like it had been for so many important moments in my life. I knew that I couldn't truly heal unless I had released all of the pain and trauma that I associated with my mother and our relationship. Although I didn't know it at the time, this would help us mend and heal.

Friends

I told my closest friends, and they were incredible and remained steadfast support for me throughout every single step of this healing journey. From my very first friend in life, my godbrother, who would watch reality TV shows with me virtually to make me laugh, to moms at school who became instant lifelong friends, this healing would not have been possible for me without the support and love of so many.

For years I have been referencing a line in one of my favorite songs that I feel explains perfectly how I feel about my friends. It's from Kanye West's song "Clique," and the line is: I have been talking to God for so long after looking at my life he is finally talking back with my clique. Thank you, Kanye, for putting into words what I have always felt in my heart.

Earlier that afternoon, my friend Michaella had come by to have tea with me and just sit. She and I have been friends since our days at Forest Grove Middle School in Worcester. Although we were not as close during our teenage years, as mothers, we ended up living just a few blocks from each other in Boston and over the years had grown very close. We shared our upbringing as well as a similar cultural connection that made for lots of laughs. Although we had shared a long history together, it was our current interests that made us even closer. We loved reading the same books and talking about them. We even traveled across the country to hear one of our favorite authors Eckhart Tolle speak about how to be in the present moment. She would be my rock in this way and a constant reminder that all we have is right now.

Sitting on the couch with her that day, I shared some things that had happened in my past that I was embarrassed about. I never had the courage to do that before. I had wanted so many times to be my true self, the one I felt inside, but I never had the courage. This diagnosis gave me the courage, and I realized that fact once I told Michaella curled up on the couch everything I had been keeping inside for so many years and she looked back at me with love and warmth in her eyes. I knew that people loved all of me, not just the personality or image. Her reaction with genuine kindness was so endearing it gave me courage. She said, "Well, you can share all of this with Oprah under the oak when you are talking about your book." I felt in my soul that she was right, and although there was no book yet, that it would be real soon enough. She saw for me what I couldn't see for myself. I was lucky to have her just sit with me that day. To be able to be vulnerable and have a safe place to land.

On Friday night, I was once again avoiding seeing my girls because I knew they would see right through me. I met my little stepsister for dinner. I had known her since she was six years old; years before our parents had gotten married. I was her Sunday school teacher, and I absolutely adored her then and we still remain very close. She is very close to my girls as well and an incredible social worker. That night we made a plan for how she could be there to support the girls. This was the most incredible gift. We sat that night and talked about how much we meant to each other and how much love we had for each other. It was a beautiful night and made our relationship even deeper. She remained steadfast with whatever the girls would need emotionally throughout. This little girl that I had taken care of so many times over the years was now taking care of me and my girls in a way that I could never really fully explain. I know a huge part of why my girls are doing so well today was because she was such a big part of supporting them.

Not Ready to Tell My Girls

Waking up the next morning after multiple glasses of rosé was probably not the best choice, but as I remembered what was happening, I sobered up within minutes. I also knew I couldn't drink anymore to numb my pain. It was real. I wasn't dreaming. I put the covers over my head like a toddler, peaked out, and confirmed that yes indeed, it was Saturday, it had been 36 hours since I received the call, and that I still hadn't told my girls. This was weighing on me so heavily because it was exactly what I had feared the most.

Having grown up with my father being so sick, my entire early life revolved around his disease. I didn't want my girls to have to worry about me that way, but here I was in that exact position facing my absolute worst fear: telling my children that I now had to deal with a disease; that this would affect everyone in our family on some level. As a mother, I was always the one steering the ship, the girls and I have very close bonds, I call it like I see it, and we have always had a very transparent relationship. I was so happy to see them taking initiative in their own lives, making decisions, and becoming independent. I was always the rock in the family: strong and helping make things happen for everyone. My energy had depleted, I was running on empty. The idea that my girls would have the same type of worry that I had at their age made me so sad.

On Saturday, September 7th, I would receive so much guidance that would really allow my healing to happen.

My husband was working that day and had left very early in the morning to drop off our youngest daughter, Thalia, who had a cross-country race that day. I was waiting to tell the girls together—I didn't want to have one keep it from the other. So that meant I had to wait until Sunday. That presented some logistical challenges—we lived in a small space and spent a lot of time together, so it was not optimal for sure to be hiding this from my older daughter, Melina, who also happens to be so intuitive that she had figured out at three years old that Santa was really Mom and Dad.

I told her that I had a "busy day," and that wasn't entirely untrue. I had some calls to make. I didn't realize at the time, but those calls would be so powerful and set the tone for my healing journey. As I would come out of my bedroom to get a snack or water, Melina would ask, "What's wrong Mom, why are you in your room making calls?" She could see right through me; she always could. My heart broke, the hardest part of all of this was my girls. Having grown up with my dad being so sick, I didn't want them to have that experience ever—in fact, it was my worst fear. I brushed her off and quickly went back into my room and closed the door. I didn't know what else to do. I didn't want her to hear this alone without her sister, the only other person in the world that could understand exactly what it was like. I also didn't want Thalia to be the "last" to find out and feel left out. The decision to tell them both together remains one of the best choices that I made during this time.

The first call was to the headmaster of the girls' school, who is an incredible woman that I have such respect and love for. I wanted to make sure that the girls would be supported at school. Not knowing anything more about what my healing would entail, I knew in my heart, without a doubt, that my girls would be nurtured and supported at their school. In fact, it's the reason I chose the school for them. In my early twenties, I would drive by their school on my way to visit my friend who was a student at Boston College, and I would wonder what type of girls were lucky enough to go there. It looked like a warm place, and I was just drawn to it, unsure why exactly. I didn't know much more about it than I had a good feeling about it.

I followed that feeling, and nearly 20 years later, my daughters both enrolled at the school, and it was everything I could have hoped for and more. In fact, when Melina was applying, the admissions department had reached out to me and suggested that we consider having her repeat fifth grade. This took my husband and me by surprise as she was an excellent student. They then explained that they felt it would be best to give her more time to blossom and then they said, "You are going to walk into our office junior year and say this is the best decision we ever made." Well, they were right, but for multiple reasons. Melina is indeed thriving in every way, but I could have never imagined how true their prediction would be. I received my diagnosis on the second day of her junior year. Indeed, it was the best decision we ever made because both our girls were loved and supported at school beyond anything I could have dreamed of.

When I spoke with their headmistress, she was incredible beyond anything I could have ever dreamed. What she shared with me during our talk gave me a clear path. I was confused, upset, and exhausted. But her words touched me to the core of my soul. They were haunting because they were exactly how I felt, yet I never knew how to express it or solve it for that matter. She told me that I needed to learn how to be loved. That struck a chord so deep that I could feel the vibration in my gut. I knew she was right. I was really good at loving others, but I really sucked at loving myself. She assured me by saying that my husband would rise to the occasion, that my daughters would rise to the occasion. That gave me so much hope.

Next, she told me how on Monday, she would take both girls to the school chapel and that she would light a candle for me and keep it lit until I was healed—and she did. I would go to the school chapel for various reasons during the next ten weeks—back-to-school night or just to sit before watching my daughter's cross-country race—and seeing my lit candle there brought me so much comfort. This touched me deeply, knowing that this incredible community that we were part of stepped right in with love and warmth to support all of us. This incredible woman then shared that she was going to send a relic home with the girls that would be mine as long as I needed it. To hold it in the middle of the night if I had trouble sleeping and that it would bring me great comfort. It did that and so much more. I felt so warm and cared for after speaking to her, and since I was so overcome with gratitude, I couldn't think of a better time to tell her how I describe her to others because of how incredible she is. I shared that I often described her to people as "If Oprah and Jesus had a baby, it would be her." I then explained I am sure her parents were very nice people as well, but Jesus and Oprah are a whole other level. We both laughed, but I assured her that it is indeed how I felt, still grateful that I hadn't lost my humor. I then told my husband that he could never mention the tuition expense again as you simply couldn't buy this, and although this is one of the most expensive independent schools in the country, I felt they weren't charging enough. He agreed.

Spiritual Roots

My second call that day would change the shape of this journey. As you know by now, I grew up in Worcester, Massachusetts, in a very active Greek Orthodox community that was the foundation for most of my childhood relationships. When I was nine years old, there was lots of excitement rippling throughout our community. We had great news, a new young priest, Father Dean, and his family were coming to serve at our parish. This was met with so much hope and anticipation, and for good reason. They were everything we could have imagined and more. I remember the very first moment I met them. They lived down the street and around the corner from us. We went to their house to welcome them, and to our joy, we found a beautiful young mother chasing after her two toddlers; you could feel their warmth and it was infectious.

In the kitchen of their house, I noticed that there was a basket in the corner with a bit of movement. As I looked down into it, two huge beautiful brown eyes looked back at me with wonder—it was a baby in a basket! I had never seen anything like this before, and it made me happy to see this amazing little baby in a basket. I could feel an instant connection to the whole family; however, there was something special about this little baby. Her energy drew me to her immediately. And 38 years later, nothing has changed. We remain so close, I was their babysitter for many years, even passing my neurosis about cleaning and other things down to them.

It was an interesting time in my family's life when I met Christen, this baby in a basket, and her family. My father was three years into his grueling battle with progressive MS, my little sister was just three years old, and my mother was very stressed. Everyone was doing their very best, but the situation was not good. I think Father Dean saw that and gave me an opportunity. He and his wife would hire me to watch their children on Saturday evenings. I was so excited because I would imagine that it was my house and they were my little kids. I loved taking care of others, and this was the perfect scenario. They were the sweetest, kindest little kids who were always so happy to see me. They taught me so much and accepted me the way I was. I think they were the first to do that ever. Caring for them just a couple of hours per week made us form a bond. I loved them immediately and still do. I couldn't have imagined Christen, whom I babysat so many years ago, would become a vital part of my healing. A true godsend. An angel.

I messaged her on Saturday morning, and she immediately answered. Once I heard her voice, I felt a sense of peace. I had just helped her about a year before when she was going through something; I had suggested a diet change and Transcendental Meditation (TM) in order for her to feel her very best, and she had adapted those and was thriving. I told her about my diagnosis and asked for her guidance. I said, "Now the teacher has become the student, please help me." She did and remains a true source of deep love with no strings attached. The pureness of her heart and soul shines through in her every word. I was so happy to hear her voice. Although we stay in touch all the time, it's always through messages. I told her right away about my diagnosis and asked for her help. For some reason that I couldn't explain, I knew she had a message for me, something I hadn't heard of or thought of yet.

I was a very avid reader now that audiobooks had become a thing. I had always struggled to read conventionally. I read very slowly and had to reread things multiple times in order for me to understand. I had lived my whole life like that. I was a poor student, and no matter how hard I worked, I just couldn't stay focused on what I was reading. So when audiobooks became available, I couldn't get enough, I realized I loved to learn, but I was just not great at traditional reading.

Because I was on a spiritual journey two years prior to my diagnosis, I was reading in addition to business books, lots of spiritual and self-help books. Actually, the reason I decided to learn and practice TM was because of a few paragraphs in a business book I was listening to almost two years prior. It was such a defining moment in my life that I remember it as if it were frozen in time. I was in the parking lot of my daughters' school waiting to pick them up from their sports practice. It was a crisp December night and dark already, even though it was not too late. It was the first week of December in 2017. I was listening to *Principles* by Ray Dalio, and in this chapter, he was describing how he had received a diagnosis and was told to get his life in order, and that was it. He then went on to explain that he had been practicing TM for 40 years and what a huge benefit this was to him, especially during this time.

He went on to explain that he was now well and that everything had worked out with his health and how grateful he was for TM and how it had helped him. I had been curious about this type of meditation since my friend Sara had mentioned that she practiced a similar technique and how it helps her. It was all I needed to hear. I was ready. I reached for my phone and did a Google search for a location close to me where I could learn this meditation. I found a teacher within minutes, it was so easy, and that is exactly how it would remain, easy and effortless. I had tried to meditate so many times and in so many different ways before, but nothing had worked for me yet until this. It was easy.

As so many Bostonians are, I am of the mindset that anything across the Charles River is a different country. If you had explained to me a week ago that I would have to go to Cambridge, Massachusetts, four days in a row, I would have told you there was no way I would have done that unless my life depended on it. Well, now looking back, it did. I truly followed my instinct, which had never steered me wrong. I knew that I was supposed to be there in Cambridge, learning this at that exact moment in time. Fast forward two years later, and it was one of the most important tools in my toolbox for my healing. I was so grateful that I still have that. It transcends everything and brings me to a place of calm, even in the middle of a storm. I am forever grateful for my friend Sara who planted the seed and for Ray Dalio sharing his experience. Learning TM was the greatest gift that I have ever bought myself.

Hearing Christen affirm that TM was a game-changer for her in her healing journey as well as other wellness information around diet, she also mentioned that there was one more piece that had helped her. She said that she had been seeing this woman named Apollonia who had helped her and that she thought I would really connect with her and that she was a very incredible woman who would help me heal. At that exact moment, I knew that I had to go see this woman. There was no doubt in my mind that I was being drawn to her. I didn't even know what Apollonia would do for me, but I knew I needed to go. I asked Christen to share her contact information, and while I was still speaking to Christen, I messaged this woman who would change my life. Within moments, this angel woman messaged me back, and we arranged a time to meet on Tuesday, September 10th. It was so simple and effortless. Although she was in New York and I live in Boston, I knew I was going to see her.

The third call that day was to my daughter's godmother. She and I had been raised together, as our families are very close A loyal and kind person, I knew she would be there for me and my family, no matter what. We had been through all of our life moments together, and this one would be no different. She remained a quiet, thoughtful, and supportive sounding board for me and still is.

That Saturday evening, my husband and I had plans to meet old friends for dinner. Still in shock, we kept our plans and decided to go. We made it through the whole dinner, catching up about summer, our travels, and children like usual. Toward the end of the evening, I could no longer hold it in. I casually mentioned that I had just been diagnosed with breast cancer. Like I was ordering dessert or something—I just didn't know what else to do. They were so shocked. I could see that my husband was not happy I had shared the news. He was sitting very closed off again, just like the first night. Our friends were so kind and stayed talking with us until the restaurant was ready to close. I shared with them my whole story and how scared I was, I had been trembling since Thursday night. She took my hand and assured me with her warm and loving way that she would be there for anything I needed. That gave me so much comfort, and I felt an instant closeness to her. Although we had been friends and former neighbors for years, I felt a whole new love for her at that moment.

The Courage to Tell My Girls I Have Cancer

When I woke up Sunday morning, I was more nervous than ever. I had planned on telling the girls that day. In my mind, I had organized to the best of my ability what I wanted to say so it would go well. My friend Julia had given me some insights about what to say a few days earlier. I thought it was so good I called her that morning to coach me. She suggested that I tell them what I have and that I was in the best possible hands and that I was going to get through this. I wanted to be honest with them, but also not scare them, which was hard to do because I was so scared myself. I had asked Joy to come over to help my husband and me tell the girls. They are very close to her as well and trust her, and I thought it would bring them additional comfort in case I lost it. I knew there was a potential that I could break down in front of the girls right when I was telling them. My husband wasn't showing any emotion around this, so I knew I needed another adult with me to deal with whatever reaction was coming.

I was shaking; this was one of the hardest things I have ever had to do. I explained what the doctors had told me and asked if they had any questions. They were both staring back at me, and then Thalia said, "Well, you are being very vague, so I'm not sure what to ask." So I decided to try again. I put aside everything I had rehearsed and just spoke from my heart. I think they could feel how vulnerable I was being. I no longer wanted to hide how I felt to anyone, including my children.

I assured them that I was going to get through this, which I truly believed. I knew no matter what the medical information was, I was going to keep getting up each day, putting one foot in front of the other and just keep going. Even if that meant some days while they were at school I would cry my eyes out all day and then clean myself up before they got home. I couldn't pretend that

I was okay; I couldn't put a fake smile on and cover up my fear. All I could do was show up, get up each day and try again. That's it. I wanted to show them that life carries on, so right after I told them about the cancer, I went to have brunch with Joy and our close friends, which was usual for a Sunday. I had arranged for my stepsister to spend the afternoon with the girls in case they had questions that they weren't comfortable asking me. I knew in order for me to start to heal that I couldn't focus on anyone else, including my daughters. This was the first time in my life that I was only thinking about myself. I made sure that they had the support they trusted while I figured out how to take care of myself for the first time in my life.

MRI Day

The next day, I was scheduled to have an MRI at five o'clock in the evening to see if there were any more spots. I was petrified. Literally shaking uncontrollably. How was I going to get through the day? My husband had left for work, my daughters had left for school, and I was in bed, devastated and crying alone, a loud primal cry that echoed through our whole apartment. I cried so many tears that the sheets had gotten wet and were now cold against my skin. My room was dark and cold, the energy was off, and I was feeling entirely sorry for myself. I wanted to die at that moment.

Then, like an angel, my housekeeper appeared over me. She took me in her arms like I was a small child, she pressed her cheek against mine, and she whispered to me, "Wake up Jo, it's time to wake up." I could feel her energy vibrating all around me, I could feel her love for me, and at that moment, that's what gave me the strength to go on. She then took out a bright green top from my closet and told me to take a shower and get dressed and to walk outside. She said it was a beautiful day and that I had to go outside immediately. I listened to her as if I were a small child. I showered, put on my bright green shirt, and did my best to stop my trembling legs.

Every Monday for years, Michaella and I would go to a SoulCycle class. We had met such a wonderful group of women there. It was so refreshing because we are all at different phases of our lives, ranging from women whose children are already married to young mothers of toddlers. The reason we had all come together so naturally was because the class was taught by Sara. I knew from the very first moment that I had taken Sara's class four years ago that she was special. There was an incredible energy around her, and I could just feel that she was going to be such an incredible light in my life. Our friendship outside of SoulCycle had grown over the years, and I was so grateful to have such a nice young woman in my life to watch evolve and grow.

I was too upset to go to class that day, so I called her and left her a message asking for her help. I described the current situation, and I told her that I had an MRI later that day at five o'clock and asked if she could think of me during her 5:30 class that evening and to send energy to me at that time. When she called me back, I could hear that she was crying and so upset by my news. We spoke for a while, and I told her I really needed her love and support to get through this, especially today. In her quiet and thoughtful way, while holding back tears, she assured me that she would be with me every step of the way.

A few of my closest friends had arranged to meet me for breakfast; they were like angels anticipating what I needed before I even knew. As we sat around the table, I was visibly distraught and shaking. I could barely get any food down. I kept telling my friends how upset I was about everything in my life; my marriage was in such a bad place. I felt so devastated by everything going on in my personal life that this diagnosis was just too much for me to process. I was sick of feeling this way, and now I was actually sick. My friends encouraged me to put this to the side and to focus on healing my body. The problem is that I knew that without acceptance of my marriage as it was currently and moving on from the past that I had absolutely no chance in healing my body. I could no longer approach anything with the same reaction that I had in the past. I would get so angry and upset and lash out at my husband and myself. I knew that there had to be a different way forward. Perhaps it wasn't my husband that was making me feel this way; maybe it was me.

After leaving that breakfast, I felt for the first time ever that perhaps I should surrender and start to think of myself only and see where that would lead me. I had never felt that way before. I walked to my husband's office, which was a block away, went upstairs, and waited for him in his back office until he had a break between patients. I looked at him, hugged him, and said I wanted to try, really try, to put our past behind us and to start over. That was the first step in our healing. Although there were many setbacks during the next ten weeks, at that moment, I could feel that our energy had started to shift, so we were at least walking on the same road. It was a start. A miracle. When I walked outside on that beautiful bright sunny September day, I felt lighter. A small sense of relief came over me, and for that I was grateful.

I had reached out to one of my friends from church who is a mentor to me. I was so grateful to have my community behind me, but at the same time, I couldn't handle communicating with people directly. I wanted prayers and support but didn't want to answer my phone or texts. So by reaching out to one, I knew she could organize all of our church friends in prayer. She immediately went into action, and within a couple of hours, I could feel the energy and love around me. Even though I hadn't spoken to them, I could feel them with me.

My mother came in to visit with me. We had had a very challenging relationship for my entire life. I did feel that in order for me to heal, I had to tell her things that I had been holding back and lying about for years. Although so many times I had wanted to tell her in the past, I was never brave enough. That day over tea, I told her things that had been burdening my soul for many years. I was honest with her without worry. At that moment, looking into her eyes, in an instant she became the mother I always needed. She took my hand and told me everything was okay and that I had done the best I could. I could feel her love, and at that moment, I started to forgive myself too. This caring moment from my mother was the catalyst for me to start really loving myself. I had so much guilt and never felt good enough. I felt that day, she really saw me for who I was for the first time.

The time was nearing for my MRI, and I was very nervous. My husband was taking me, and I was grateful. I had never relied on him for anything like this. Even when I was in labor with our daughters, I had accepted that his work schedule was always the priority and had done most things on my own. This was the first time that I had become the priority of his time. In fact, I had always told him every time he had asked, "Would you like me to cancel my patients and go with you?" I would say, "No, don't worry." This time, I didn't even ask. He said, "I have moved around my schedule and I am taking you to your MRI." This was an incredible act of kindness, and it softened how I saw him. This was the start of a big shift in our relationship.

We walked to the MRI imaging in the hospital, and I was not in a good mental place. I was so glad to have my husband with me. He filled out all the tedious paperwork and tried to keep me calm. I am not comfortable in closed spaces, so I was nervous about the actual test, aside from being nervous about the actual results—a double stress situation. I was told that I would have to remove all my jewelry and was prepared, even bringing a little travel case and screwdriver to remove the two love bracelets that I have worn for years on my right arm. My husband took the screwdriver and tried for 20 minutes to remove them, but with no luck. He had taken these off for me multiple times over the years, but on that particular day, they were both stuck.

I saw this as my way out of this test—I was already so nervous that I jumped at the chance to reschedule. I immediately got up, went to the front desk, and was talking my way out of it. I was very good at getting what I wanted, but that day I just couldn't make it happen. I felt my phone buzzing in my pocket and when I looked at the number, I saw it was from one of the doctor's offices. When I answered, I realized it was the breast surgeon that my doctor had recommended, telling me that in order for me to be seen that Thursday, I would need to have the MRI right now. Well, that made me even more upset because now I knew that if I didn't have it done, I couldn't see the surgeon, and the bracelets were still stuck on me. As soon as the tears were welling up in my eyes, this young woman that worked for the imaging department came up to me, calmly took my hand, looked at my bracelets, and assured me that I would be okay and that these particular bracelets wouldn't interfere with the imaging. There was no turning back now!

I looked at my phone before handing it to my husband and saw I had a text from Sara. She had sent me her playlist for the 5:30 class, and her text read: You go right in and we will be right behind you. As I looked up at the clock, I realized that because of the delay, it was almost 5:30. I kissed my husband and went into the prep room. I knew that the energy of Sara's class would be with me, and I never looked back. I felt an instant courage. The super-nice MRI technician said she could play music for me inside the machine, so I selected Ed Sheeran. I closed my eyes and imagined I was in the SoulCycle class, listening to every song as if I was on the bike. I pictured myself like I had been hundreds of times before, trying to stay on the beat and climbing the hill. On the last song, I started to cry like I often do during a SoulCycle class. It was a song that reminds me of my father. I truly felt that I was in the class that day, that all of the collective energy from Sara and her riders was with me every single step of the way.

In the car on the way home, I took out my phone to text Sara and thank her, but when I looked at the playlist she had sent over earlier, I was in complete shock. Four of the same songs had been played during my MRI and in the exact same order as they were in class. I had chills all over my body, knowing what I had just experienced was incredibly special and such a gift.

REFLECTIONS ON HEALING

Who Do You Call?

When you get the initial phone call, it's like an out-of-body experience. At least that's what it felt like for me.

My husband was the first person I called, and since I was still in shock myself, I just told him. This was just seconds after I hung up with my doctor because I was worried about my girls coming home from school. So, it will depend on where and when you get the news. If you are in your doctor's office, you may have more time to process before calling anyone. I had to think fast because of the timing.

If you are married, my suggestion is to tell your spouse first. Regardless of the struggles my husband and I were having, there was a reason we were still together, and I wanted to respect that. Although at the time I didn't have time to think about it, as I now reflect back, I am grateful that he was the first person I called. This also set the tone for our relationship healing. Do what feels right for you and what you feel you need at the moment. Keep things as simple as you can.

My next call was to Joy. If you have that person in your life that you can call no matter what, then call them. This was really helpful for me to have the time with my husband and my friend so that I could process before telling my family, children, and friends. Take as long as you need. Everyone is different, and every case is different. You know how people are in your life. If it's going to bring you more stress by telling them, then don't right now. You are just trying to accept this yourself. Take the time you need.

Telling Your Parents

This is tough. As a parent myself, this is one of the worst things I could ever imagine hearing. Be kind and thoughtful, but do not fall into the role of managing their fear. I found it helpful to have my sister take on that role with my mother. Your parents are, of course, worried about you; you can't now be worried about them being worried about you. It can turn into a tricky situation. If you have someone who can help you by being a buffer between you and your parents, this is great. This was particularly helpful in our family dynamic and helped me avoid a lot of potentially emotional exchanges that I just didn't have the energy for. This was a very big part of my healing. Allowing my sister to step in and be there for my mother during this initial time was one of the best decisions I made. You simply don't have the energy to handle others' fears and emotions because you can barely handle your own.

Telling Your Children

This was the absolute hardest day. My own fears and anxiety from my childhood, living with a sick parent who died, all came flooding back. I took some time here. I thought about what I could say to my daughters that would be clear and loving but not scare them. Then I realized they were going to be scared no matter what. And that my childhood was not their story. This would now be part of their life's story. That was the hardest part for me to overcome. I took a few days here, talked to a friend who had given me great advice, and practiced what I was going to say. Because they are close in age, I told them at the same time because I didn't want Melina to have the burden of keeping it from Thalia. I told them the truth, I showed strength and vulnerability, I was myself.

Take the time you need. Don't rush yourself. You know your children better than anyone. You know what they need. Keep it as simple as you can. All children want to know is that you are going to be okay. This is hard to reassure them when you don't know yourself. So focus on what you do know. Make that as positive as possible. Keep the information clear and simple. Make sure you point out the good things. A few of these could be:

- I love my doctor, and I am in such good hands.
- I am healthy in every other way, and this will help me.
- There are so many women who have had this, and they go on to live long, healthy lives.
- I feel good about my options.
- God is with me, and I feel taken care of.

Making sure your children have support outside of you and your husband is key. You are going to be so busy focusing on what you need to do, and your husband or partner will have to take on more of your role when possible. My girls also had the support of their aunt, my sister, who was there for them when I couldn't be. This was a huge help. If you have a friend or family member who can come in and help in that way, this is very valuable. Their school was also a huge support; knowing what was going on, they stepped in as a second family. Whatever you have access to and feel comfortable with, do that. It could be a family member, a neighbor, a coach, a babysitter, a friend. Think about a person your child already has a good relationship with and reach out and ask them to help you and be there for things that will come up. These things could be a simple ride to something or just when you need a mental break, and they could take them out for lunch or an ice cream. This will be extremely helpful. This will give your children the comfort they need when you can't give it to them.

I know it can be hard to ask for help, but this is the time. Especially when it involves your children. Accept the help.

Telling Family Members

I found comfort in telling my siblings. Even though my sister and I had had a strained relationship, I always felt close to her as well as to my stepbrother and stepsister. They were easy and supportive on many levels: managing my parents, helping with my children, and being there for me. They were a big part of my healing journey.

If you have a strained relationship with a sibling or family member, this is not the time to rehash it. Do not bring past stress into your life. Every family is different. Do whatever feels right for you. Remember, there is no right or wrong here, and if you know people are not capable of letting things go and they will bring you more stress, no need to tell them, even if they are your siblings. You also don't need to explain yourself to anyone about the decisions you make here. If someone brings it up, disengage—there is simply no need. You don't have the time or energy to deal with this now, so don't. It's a choice. This is 100% completely your call. Follow your gut. Regardless of what you decide to do here, remember that holding on to hurt is also hurting you. If you are in a toxic situation with a sibling that will add stress to your life, treat it like you would a past trauma. Follow the four steps: Identify, Accept, Bless, Forgive. This is something you can do privately for yourself. It will help keep any past family drama away.

Telling Your Friends

Okay, this is a big one. In my experience, there are two ways to go here. One is to keep it to a very small group, and the other is to share it with a larger circle. Do what you feel is right for you. Do not tell people out of obligation or because you are afraid you will hurt their feelings. This is your journey. People who love you will understand, no matter what.

If you decide to keep it very small, just a couple of friends, this has many benefits. You have the ability to keep your life more "normal" because fewer people know. You won't have to answer questions about it through-out the day, and this can be nice. The challenge of this can be that if you need to talk about it, they might not be available exactly when you need them. I have seen people do this, and it works really well. It depends on your personality and friend group dynamic.

If you decide to go larger and open it up like I did it, there are many benefits but also challenges. The benefits are there is always someone available, no matter what.

This was really helpful for me because I am a person who likes to communicate. That same communication was, at times, extremely overwhelming. A few weeks into my diagnosis, I decided that with a larger group of family and friends, I would send out updates when I had them and asked people to please not message me individually. It got too overwhelming for me to be communicating individually with each person. This was very helpful and worked well. I asked people to please send cards or notes but not texts with questions. The overwhelming love and support I received was some-thing that I will cherish forever. It gave me the strength I needed at some of the hardest moments. I have saved every single card or note, and I will forever.

There is no right or wrong here. Just do what feels right for you. Take a little time if possible, and think about what you think would make you feel more comfortable and do that. Don't beat yourself up about what other people might be feeling. This is a delicate time for you, and you need peace and calmness.

Tell Your Close Fiends You Need Support

Don't assume people know what you need. I know it sounds simple, but it's super important. Be detailed and clear, especially with friends who can take the direction. For example, On October 4th, when I was waiting alone all day for the results that never came, I could have made plans to break up the day so I wasn't alone. When you are waiting for results, try not to be alone. If you are at work, make sure a coworker knows to check in on you during the day. If you are not comfortable sharing this at work, book times throughout the day to talk with people who know and support you. If possible, arrange to meet a friend for tea or lunch during your break. You don't need to wait alone. This will make you feel better.

It Is Safe to Be Vulnerable

It's okay to show people that you are scared. You don't always need to keep it all together. If it feels right to call a friend and cry, do it. Reveal your whole self. This will allow you to release the "image" you have of yourself. This will also enable you to decompress by taking all of the pressure off to appear a certain way. We all get stuck in roles that we fill in all relationships. Take a relationship where you have been the one that was mostly giving advice and ask that person to help you. They will, and it's so nice. There is great comfort in this because it brings the relationship to another level.

Chapter Two:
Heaven in Harlem

My Father's Spirit

That Tuesday, Joy and Michaella had arranged to take me to see Apollonia, the woman that Christen had insisted I see in New York who had been so helpful to her on her healing journey. So the three of us ventured off to see this woman who we knew nothing about. I knew that I had to go see her, I had no idea what she was going to do to help me, but I just knew that she would.

When I was getting ready to go to the airport, I reached out to my aunt, my father's only sister. Our families had been estranged since my father's death almost 30 years ago. I had reconnected with her a few years earlier, and we had kept in touch. When she answered the phone, I was calm but also very clear that I didn't want to talk about the whole situation, but I needed her help. Through our conversations, I had realized that she remained very close to my father's spirit. I was a bit upset with my father—at the time, I couldn't reach him like I had been able to almost daily. I asked her to ask him to help and protect me. I knew that she would continue to ask for this without my prompting.

My father had been such a big presence in my life from the moment of his death, but in this, my hardest moment, I felt angry and that he had let me down. I never shared these feelings with anyone; my relationship with him and his spirit has always been very deep. I could feel his presence with me before, but on this day I just couldn't. This was a first for me. From the day of his funeral, when I was 16 years old, I could feel him near me in spirit. So now, I was mad at him. How could he let this happen to me? Hadn't I been through enough? These emotions stayed with me for some time.

I have lived with the emotional impact of my father's sickness and passing for the past 30 years. It was a big part of how I identified myself—always living in fear that something would happen to me like it had happened to my dad. Now I felt like everything I had worried about was happening. I knew that I needed to release that old story I kept telling myself and everyone else. It was time for a big change. I was ready to move on from the past. Now I had to figure out a new way to keep my father's spirit with me without it becoming overwhelming. Apollonia would be the one to help me do that.

We pulled up to Logan airport on this overcast day for our flight to New York. I had traveled to New York many times before, and most of those times with Joy. We would go for shopping trips and fabulous lunch and dinners, but this time was different. Instead of planning out my perfect outfit, making sure we had the most fabulous lunch reservation, I instead was shaking uncontrollably and just an overall wreck.

Angels All Around Me

I am usually the organizer of these trips, telling everyone where we'd be going and at what time. I am a meticulous organizer and love doing this. Not on that Tuesday. I was so grateful to have my friends with me guiding me and taking care of me. The trip had started off with great ease and grace. It was just one of those days when the security line moved fast, and everyone we came into contact with was so kind and friendly. It was a clear indication of how the day would go.

Once we had passed security and got to our gate, we realized we had some extra time, so I thought we should walk to the lounge and see if we could get in. We were not traveling in the class that would give us access, but I just had a good feeling about it. Despite my fear and shakes, I was still a girl who liked a nice lounge. We walked up to the Delta Sky Club and handed the nice lady our boarding passes. She had the kindest, most beautiful blue eyes. She looked at me and said, "Welcome, we have been expecting you. Come right in." I have been traveling since I was a year old, and that had never happened before. It was a random act of kindness—this theme would continue throughout our whole day.

Once we boarded our flight, I could not stop my legs from shaking. My mind was racing, trying to digest everything that had happened since the phone call on Thursday. Was this really my life now? So many emotions and so much to think about. I was tired. I hadn't slept for more than two hours in a row in over three months. My heart was racing, and I felt random pain all over my body, I was shaking, and I could feel that, physically, I was shutting down. Not because of the diagnosis, but because of the free-floating fear.

I looked up, and like an angel, the flight attendant who had bright blue eyes looked at me and told me she liked my necklace, and that, although it was only ten o'clock and this was a very short flight, she would be happy to get me a glass of champagne after takeoff. We started laughing because any other time that would have been music to my ears, but today I politely said no thank you. After takeoff, they offered a snack, and much to our surprise, it was a basket of fresh fruit, exactly what I needed at that moment. I had never seen this on a shuttle from Boston to New York—another amazing gift that day that came out of nowhere.

Once we landed and were about to deplane, the same flight attendant handed me a bag. She told me I might need this later in the day and that she hoped everything was going to go well for me. I looked in the bag and it was packed with snacks and champagne and towels. This completely random act of kindness warmed my heart. She made such a difference in my life without even knowing me; I would find that over and over again throughout my healing journey, in places I would have never thought to look. So much love.

We found our driver in the lineup, and we were on our way from LaGuardia to Manhattan. We had some time before I was to meet Apollonia, so we decided to go to Barneys and have some lunch. I always loved having lunch at Barneys every time I was in New York. That day I could barely sit at the table. I was in so much distress that I couldn't settle down. The three of us sat talking, mostly my friends to each other, and I was just listening. During that conversation, I was prompted to tell them a story about Thalia losing a ring of mine while we were traveling in Vienna earlier that summer. I am not sure why it had come up, the ring really had no emotional significance or meaning. It was soon time to head to Harlem, where I was going to meet Apollonia at her apartment, still unsure of what she could do to help me.

As we drove, I was shaking so much that my friends were holding my legs down to try to help me. As we went through all the busy New York streets, we realized how, for some reason, traffic had been very light that day and that all of the lights seem to be in our favor. Again, this was a first.

We pulled onto Apollonia's street, which had an elementary school on it. It was afternoon, and school had just let out. Mothers with babies in strollers heading to pick up their older children just like the three of us had so many times before—this brought up so much emotion in me. I thought about all the days I had picked up my girls from school, rushing from work to be on time or fighting traffic, and how sometimes I was so overwhelmed by the stress that was going on inside me, and I would try really hard to hide from them what was going on. I also thought about all the sweet times when the weather was nice, and they were little, and I would take them to the playground or for an ice cream after school. How quickly the years had passed, and yet on so many of the hard days, it felt like the day would never end.

Seeing My Soul

We buzzed the apartment number, and there was no answer. I stood there, and for a minute thought, Have we come all this way and she's not here? Had I mixed up the time? As soon as all these doubts started to creep up, I could feel that the energy around us was changing. I looked over my shoulder and saw this beautiful woman walking very quickly toward us. She smiled the warmest smile, and immediately I knew that was her. We walked up the four flights of stairs and into her bright and warm home. It felt safe and welcoming; I was happy to be there. Joy and Michaella sat on the couch, and I sat at the table opposite Apollonia. I started to tell her about my diagnosis and the reason I was there, hoping she could heal me. I could see that she had a very special gift, just by the way she was looking at me. It was as if she was looking past my body and could see my soul.

She told me that she doesn't heal people, but that she helps people heal themselves. I was a bit disappointed when I heard that because I was looking for someone to fix this, to take me out of the pain I was in. But I realized she was right. I had told so many people this before, making statements like "everything we need to heal is within us," and I believed what I was saying, it was just hard to apply to myself. I trusted her, and I opened my mind to this.

After asking me a few questions, she asked me what I had lost in Vienna that previous summer. I was in shock. Only about an hour earlier, I had mentioned to Joy and Michaella about the lost ring, no one other than my daughters and I knew about the ring. This caught my attention. She also asked me about the left side of my face and if I had a problem there. I had a tooth there that had had a root canal several years ago, but my husband, who is also my dentist, had just looked at my teeth, and I had no issues. This would come up a few weeks later in a way that was so shocking that it was almost unbelievable.

She then took me into a room to treat me. The room was very calming and simple. I laid on the floor like she asked. It's still very hard for me to explain exactly what happened during those two and a half hours that she treated me, but it was life-changing and the start of my transformation. She placed her hand above my left thigh by my lower abdomen and asked what had happened there. I couldn't believe it. I had had a hernia operation when I was two years old on that exact spot. This sent shivers down my spine. She asked why I had had that operation, and I told her that my mother had told me that I was crying so hard that I had given myself a hernia. She was surprised by my answer and told me that I should ask my mother about this.

Over the next two and a half hours she would place her hands or hover them over certain parts of my body. My body would involuntarily react by twitching or spasming. I started to feel a huge release. Tears were streaming out of my eyes, but they were falling to the side toward my ears. I have cried hundreds of times before, but this was different—not one tear went down my cheeks. I started to speak and say the names of the saints that my children and some of my godchildren were named for. I wasn't thinking about what I was saying, the words were just coming out. I had never felt this way before. I couldn't understand what was happening. Then I started to repeat the name Michael over and over, unsure why. It would be weeks later, on November 4th, that I would fully understand what the significance of that was.

With Apollonia's help, I started to release all that I had been holding onto for my entire life that no longer served me. This session was just the beginning. I knew I had a lot more work to do. I committed that day to do everything I had to do to align my soul with my physical body. I knew that I had been splintered for some time, and if I wanted to really heal from this disease, I would have to dig deep and start on the inside. I decided that day in Harlem that I would do the work, like really do the work, to let go and forgive and find acceptance with my past and in the present moment.

When I walked out of the room, Joy and Michaella stared at me in disbelief; I looked like a completely different person, but the real change was on the inside. I had stopped shaking, I felt peaceful, and my eyes had light behind them again. To my amazement, I looked in the mirror, and although I had been crying for the entire session, my face looked fresh and my eyes were peaceful, not puffy or swollen.

I didn't realize how much time had passed and how long I had been in there. It was like nothing I had ever experienced before. That session changed the course of my healing and my life. I would work with Apollonia throughout the next ten weeks, and we would go deep into my past and my life. I know this is a major part of why I was able to heal and prepare for my surgery.

Finding Inner Peace

We had arranged to have dinner and meet another close friend who had been in New York on business that day. This was one of my very first friends I made when I had become a mother nearly 18 years ago, so it was special to have her with me on that day. We would all drive back to Boston that evening together. We went to dinner at one of my favorite restaurants Le Bilboquet where I have celebrated so many fun and happy occasions. This was a beautiful night filled with wonderful food and good friends. On our drive home that night, I sat quietly, reflecting on the day and how beautiful it had been. How many things happening to help me without effort. I could hear that my friends were talking, but I was in my own world.

We had been on the road for a couple of hours and hadn't stopped once, not for a red light or traffic or anything, and it stayed that way all the way to Boston. I was hopeful that this was how my future would be, just like this drive back from New York— smooth and easy.

Once we approached Boston, my friends were each dropped off at their homes. Eventually, I was alone in the car with the one who lived closest to me. I looked at her and said without thinking that if the MRI revealed anything else, I would opt for a double mastectomy, without hesitation. It's as if I knew what was ahead.

That night as I pulled up to my building, it was past midnight. I rarely come home that late. The concierge, a very kind man who has known me for years, looked at me with concern and asked me what was wrong. I told him what had happened and that I was just coming back from New York. He wrote down on a piece of paper a name of a prayer line that I could call in the morning to ask them to pray for me. It was such a sweet gesture. When I looked at the name, I was shocked because it was one of the names I had been repeating during the session I had with Apollonia earlier that day. I thanked him and took the paper. There were so many incredible miracles that day.

That night I slept so peacefully for the first time in three months.

REFLECTIONS ON HEALING

Unpack Your Emotional Baggage

Forgive yourself now! What are you waiting for? This is the time ....

If you have something in your past you are ashamed of, this is definitely the time to release that. Call a trusted friend and arrange to see them. Then tell them what's on your mind. Before you tell them, think about what you want to gain by releasing this to them. If you want them to give you feedback, then let them know that in advance. If you want them to listen and tell you it's all okay and to give you a hug, then tell them that in advance. Pick a friend who is compliant and capable of taking that direction. This is very freeing and will give you a sense of peace.

Be Open-Minded

The amount of information out there is overwhelming and stressful. Focus on successful people you look up to, whether you know them or not, and see what they do that brings them peace and balance. If it works for them, there's a great chance it will work for you. Pick one practice that three of them have in common and do that. This is the perfect time to learn something new that will help you. It could be meditation, journaling, prayer, yoga, a morning routine—anything that you don't already do. Don't overthink it, keep it simple, commit to adding it, and just do it.

Identify Your Positive-Thinking People

Surround yourself with people who are positive. The last thing you need is people to pile on stress. Be very aware of who you let in at this time. You don't have any room for negative anything. You are already saying this stuff in your own head. I know people agreeing with you feels good at the moment, but it doesn't help you. If you have people in your life who are the first to RSVP to a pity party, do not interact with them now. Protect yourself from people who will sit around with you and feed your sad story.

Look Outside Your Daily Circle for Support

Think about the people you have in your life who are not part of your daily routine. Most of us have friends who are around our age and at similar stages of life. Bringing new energy into this journey is very helpful. Reaching out to younger people is useful because they have a different perspective and tools that could help you. The same goes for older people. This is extremely comforting because they have more life experience.

Chapter Three:
The Jo Inside

The Longest Day

I woke up on that Wednesday morning, and for the first few minutes, I couldn't recognize where I was. I had slept so deeply and without waking up, this was a new feeling for me. I looked around my bedroom, and everything was physically the same, but I felt different. A new wave of peace had come over me. My body was wrapped up in the crisp sheets, and I could see the sunshine peeking out from the corner of the window that wasn't covered by the blackout shades. The house was quiet; I had no idea what time it was. I remember thinking if I just stay here and I don't get up and I don't see or talk to anyone, will this all just go away? That was short-lived. I knew that this day I would be receiving a call from my doctor with the results of my MRI. This had its very own separate set of anxieties.

Every time my cell phone rang, my heart sank to my stomach and my legs turned into Jell-O. And since my daughters used my cell phone number on every website, and for every online order, I must have been on 1,000 different automated telemarketing lists. I answered every single call that came in, just in case it was my doctor, only to realize that it was an automated message. This was so frustrating and painful. My anxiety level got so intense that it took time for me to recover from each call. This torture went on for the majority of the day.

I did all the things that I could do to stay in the present moment. I didn't want to get ahead of myself and create a story of all the things that could go wrong. All of the self-help books and mindful practices that I had learned in my life were within me, but I just couldn't reach them. The stress and trauma I was feeling were like nothing I had felt before. This was a whole new level of feeling out of control. Like something had come into my life and, in a split second, changed it forever. I was scared. I was lonely. I was shaken.

The hours on that day were the longest I have ever experienced. My mother and stepfather had come over to see me in the afternoon. I could barely keep a conversation together. I didn't know what I wanted. It was hard to be alone, and yet at the same time, I didn't want to be around people. I was so conflicted.

My personality was always to try to please or try to do the "right" thing, even at the expense of my own feelings. I learned in the weeks to follow how to stay true to what I felt in the moment and no longer do what was expected of me to make others feel better. This was a huge tool in my healing. I had to learn that it was not my responsibility to make any adult in my life feel okay about what I was going through. This was very hard because I always cared about what others thought of me and how they were feeling about my life. That was an eye-opening moment for me. I realized I no longer wanted to live that way. I decided to start trying to break that pattern.

On that day, I started to make my actions support what I was feeling inside. I had a long-standing very bad habit of doing things that I didn't really want to do and then spending days being mad at myself for doing that. I no longer had the time or patience for that. This was one of the first and major behavioral changes that I made, and I am so grateful that I did. I had heard about boundaries and had tried so many times in the past to implement them, but I had always caved. My guilt would overtake me and that was that. I spent so much time worrying about other people's feelings that I ignored my own. I was always so outspoken and seemed to "do whatever I wanted," but in reality, that was not the case. I was always struggling to do what was expected of me, especially where my husband and mother were concerned.

My mother and I have had a complicated relationship since I can remember. It was filled with a lot of conflict and arguing. I love my mother and she loves me, but we just couldn't get along. It was very common for us to scream at each other over the phone or in person. I know that I have a huge part in this. I am always on the defensive when I am around her. We could barely agree on anything, and the way we communicated with each other was very unhealthy. I think we both made an effort at different times throughout the years to improve this, but we always seemed to end up in the same place. I knew that this wasn't something that we couldn't fix now, so I decided to park it where it was. Accept it as it is and focus on the parts of our relationship that were working. That also meant that when I wanted to be by myself, I would say no to a visit. If I didn't want to talk on the phone, I wouldn't answer. Initially, I struggled when I made these changes. I also started to apply them to every relationship in my life. I knew this way of being no longer served me or others. It wasn't anyone's fault that I held myself to this standard.

This is something that I am currently still working on. The inner dialogue in my head is what always tries to pull me back. I am getting better at it now, and it's been one of the most positive changes in this process.

When the phone rang in the late afternoon and I realized it was my doctor, I was sitting across from my mother and stepfather, my girls were in their room, already doing homework. I answered, and my doctor shared the news. There were two more suspicious spots in the same breast, but all the lymph nodes looked good, and the other breast looked clear. I burst into tears of relief. This was great news. And for the first time in almost a week, I was able to breathe a sigh of relief.

Putting on a Happy Face

The emotions were going through me in waves. First, I was relieved that the other breast was clear and that all the lymph nodes were good. But then as I walked toward my daughters' room to share the good news with them, I froze. What did these other two spots mean? Was this more cancer? I put on a happy face for my girls, shared the news, and then went into my bathroom, closed that door, fell down onto the bath mat in front of the tub, put my hands over my face, and cried and cried. I didn't want my girls to see me so upset, especially since I just shared the "good news." I was so upset; in a matter of seconds, my emotions would go from relief to sheer panic. It felt as if I took ten steps forward, and then fell right back as if I had never walked at all. The pain and fear were ripping through me so fast it felt as if I was being beaten. I sat there on my bathroom floor in the dark, hugging myself like I would my daughters when they were upset or sick. I was scrunched up, holding my knees tight to my chest, my eyes like faucets just pouring out tears, yet I was completely silent. I sat like this for what felt like an eternity.

I heard the main door of our apartment open, and I knew that meant my husband was home from work. He always came into our bathroom to wash up and change his clothes after work, so I knew it was only a matter of minutes before he would come in and see me like this. I was relieved he was there. Despite the challenges we had had and the fact that our relationship was in such distress, he was still the only person who could bring me back from a place like this. I heard the subtle knock on the bathroom door, and then the door opened slowly, and he appeared. He had a look of confusion on his face—after all, I had called him less than an hour ago to tell him the doctor had called with the MRI results and that they were good. So naturally, he was shocked to see me in this state.

He helped pull me up and did everything he could to tell me that it was going to be okay, that those other spots were nothing, and that this was going to all be fine. I didn't want to hear it; I was still so upset. I could see in his eyes that he was scared too. We stood there in the dark bathroom, a place where we had so many arguments recently, but on that night, there was just silence. He held me as I cried. I knew right then that we had reconnected on a soul level. These glimpses of a connection I knew was possible gave me hope.

I don't think that I had ever fully allowed myself to be loved by anyone. I was always very guarded at receiving love, even from my husband and children. I was very focused on the love that I could give others and was very good at that, but I wasn't good at accepting love. I hid this really well. My outgoing, friendly personality provided the perfect cover. I would give and give and give, always the first one to want to help out, but because I didn't know how to receive, I was dying inside.

This is one of the most important things I discovered about myself during this ten-week time: I had to allow the love in. This sounds simple and easy. How lucky was I that I had all these people around me who wanted to love and take care of me? I felt like a selfish idiot; how could I not know how to be loved? This was one of the absolute hardest things I had to learn how to do. This feeling was foreign to me. I discovered very soon that it was because I had to go to the source of love, self-love. I had to learn how to truly, madly, deeply, fall in love with myself.

This would be a huge part of my journey—actually, the most important part, more important than what I could get from the outside. I had so much love in my life, but it didn't matter because I didn't know how to accept it. The best way I can describe it is that it's like having the most decadent, rich, three-layer chocolate cake with thick creamy frosting right in front of me, all for me, but each time I try to take a bite, I cannot get it in my mouth. I serve the cake to everyone else, and they all enjoy it very much, and it gives me great pleasure to watch them eat it, but I never taste this cake. I can only imagine by watching everyone who enjoys the cake that it is something special.

I didn't know exactly how I was going to do this, I was already a meditator, had a deep faith in God, had therapy and so many self-help books but still no love for myself—how could this even be possible? I spent my whole life guarded and on defense. I didn't feel good on the inside, especially about myself. I would play mistakes that I had made over and over in my head throughout the day, some of them from over 25 years ago, but to me, they would play out in my mind as if I had just made them yesterday.

I think this will be very surprising to people who know me. I am always the first one to tell people about the importance of self-love and acceptance. It's one of the foundations on which I have raised my daughters. I always seem so self-assured and appear to have it all together. Perhaps I did that my whole life so no one would look deeper to the real me inside that was suffering with so much pain and guilt. I knew that in order for me to have any chance of coming through this and being cured, I would have to change. The "perfect," all-knowing me would have to die so that my true self could be free, and I could heal inside and out. I had to surrender to love.

I didn't have a clear idea about how I was going to do this, but I had faith that it could happen. After all, I was really good at loving others, so surely this was something I was capable of doing. I would start by reminding myself to be kind and patient with myself. That was the first step. Joy had told me this hundreds of times throughout the years, but now I was ready for it. My mother also started to say this to me many times throughout this ten-week period and still does today. Hearing it from her made all the difference to me.

Ready for a New Story

The next morning, I woke up feeling anxious. That was the day I was going to meet with a breast surgeon. Although in my life up until that point I had been in such a rush to get everything done, things checked off my list, I wasn't having those same feelings about this. I had imagined that if something like this ever happened, I would want to "cut it out" immediately, so I was surprised that I didn't feel like that at all. Instead, when I walked into the hospital to meet the surgeon, I felt like I didn't belong there. I was very clear about what was going on, and I knew that I had to let the doctors take action, but something just didn't feel right.

The kind surgeon went through all of the potential scenarios, which were all dependent on the impending biopsy results from the two other "spots" that were just discovered. All of this was so incredibly overwhelming. I was holding the relic in my hand for comfort, but as she was speaking, it felt like each word was punching me in the gut. My fear had never been worse. Once I left the appointment, I could barely speak. I felt so tired, as if I hadn't slept in days. Once I got home, I undressed, put on my pajamas, and crawled into bed. As I lay on my left side, I could feel my little tumor pressing against the crisp sheets. A vivid reminder that it was there. In a few hours, it would be a week since I got the call with my diagnosis. It felt like a year. I closed my eyes and tears poured out. I cried myself to sleep.

The next morning, I woke up feeling more hopeful, although I had absolutely no idea why. Nothing had changed, no new information from the doctors, but I just had a feeling that I had to do something. I was thankful that the part of my personality that was into "fixing" things was awake. I started with my diet. I downloaded multiple audiobooks about cancer and diet and listened to them. I was so grateful for these books and for all the authors who took the time to share such valuable information from their experience with cancer. I took notes and tried to figure out the best plan for me during this time. This was a bit tricky because I was living a very healthy lifestyle when I received this diagnosis. I was eating a mostly organic diet free of gluten and processed foods and prepared most of my meals myself as I love to cook. I went to SoulCycle at least twice a week, as well as Pilates and yoga. I was in great shape physically and was always on the go. So this was confusing to me.

I decided that I would adopt a plant-based diet, free of dairy, meat, and sugar. I also researched vitamins and supplements that I could take to help me. This was not super fun, but it gave me a sense that there was at least something I could control in this out-of-control situation. I would eat like this for the next nine weeks. I was very conscious of everything I put into my mouth. I was careful about everything, from the water I drank to the salt I cooked with. This made me feel like I was doing something to help myself that I could measure each day. It gave me comfort.

I knew there were a lot of changes that needed to be made on so many levels, making this change felt good. It was one step closer to my healing.

REFLECTIONS ON HEALING

Clean Up Your Diet

There is lots of information about certain foods being linked to cancer, especially breast cancer. The books I read were very helpful. However, my diet was already so clean, there were very few changes that I had to make. I hadn't eaten gluten in years, and I decided to eliminate dairy and sugar completely as well as meat. These are things that I ate only occasionally, but out of the nine books I read on the topic, these were the common denominators in all of them. I started eating a mostly plant-based, whole food diet, reducing the amount of olive oil I used to cook. I avoided eating packaged foods. My goal was to reduce inflammation.

Take a look at what you are eating. Make the changes that feel right for you. Be careful not to add more stress to an already stressful situation. Eliminating things can be very hard emotionally. You already feel like you have given up so much, and now this. My advice is to start with one thing at a time. Sugar is a good one to start with. Making this change will give you a sense that you are doing something to help yourself. Then when you feel ready, dairy might be a good one to eliminate next. See how you feel when you do this. Making these changes and taking control of what goes into your mouth can feel empowering. Take it step by step. Just do the best you can each day. There is such an emotional attachment to food, and it can be the source of so much comfort, so do the best you can.

If you drink milk or cream in your coffee, try to replace it with a nondairy option. There are so many yummy alternatives now.

Find the Right Supplements

I added vitamins and supplements to my diet. This was tricky for me as I had never taken anything daily before. I looked at all of the different opinions out there, and again found the greatest common denominators and took those. The ones I found were vitamins C, D, B12, E, zinc, and magnesium. I ordered these on Amazon and started taking them each day. This made me feel like there was something I could do to help myself. I am sure the vitamins probably had some health benefits, but for me this was more psychological than anything. I felt so helpless, and this gave me something physical I could do easily each day to make myself feel empowered.

Try adding vitamins to your daily routine if you don't already take them. The key here is to make sure that what you are taking is of high quality. The vitamin game can be very confusing. There are a ton that look so healthy and natural, and they are not. It is important to take the time to read the labels. I know how overwhelming this can be. To make it easier for myself, whatever vitamin I decided to order, I looked at Anthony William's Medical Medium website to see which one he recommended. I trusted the research that he had done. If you have a source that you trust, use that. Trying to figure this all out yourself can be exhausting.

If you are new to taking vitamins, put out your serving the night before so they are ready to go, and take them each morning. This can give you the mental boost you need to start the day, especially when you are having a tough day.

Get A Second Opinion

I am really fortunate to live where I live for many reasons, but especially because of the medical care that is available in Boston. When I was first diagnosed, I was hesitant to get a second opinion. Although I was in a top hospital with access to top doctors, something just didn't feel right to me. Each time I walked into that hospital, I felt like I didn't belong there. I felt defeated and tired. I ignored how I was feeling and chalked it up to the fact that I was scared, but the truth was I didn't feel the connection to the team that I was put with. Coming to terms with this was a big deal for me, especially since I knew how extremely lucky I was to have access to such incredible doctors. It just didn't feel right, and I still don't know exactly why.

I was ready to go into surgery and even had signed my consent form. Then completely randomly, a woman at my church who wasn't fully aware of my situation suggested I go see a medical naturopath named Dr. Ellis, who had helped many people heal from breast cancer. I was intrigued. I immediately reached out to him and found out he had a three-month waitlist. But something told me to call back in a few hours, and I did. They had just had a cancelation for the following Saturday, which I immediately took. Going to see Dr. Ellis was a shift in my journey. He was so kind and had so much experience. He suggested that I have another look at a different hospital. Perhaps he could sense that I was so nervous. Although I had heard it a few times from a few friends, something that day just clicked, and I knew I had to look for another team.

I reached out to a friend who had offered to help if I ever decided to have a second opinion as well as a friend who is a top oncologist, and they both immediately came back with the same recommendation. They connected me personally with Dr. Michelle, and within 24 hours I had an appointment to see her. I could tell even from the little e-mail interaction that I had with her that this was the surgeon I was supposed to be with. Miracles literally happened so that I could see this doctor. One huge one, aside from the fact that I could get an appointment so fast and I was lucky enough to live down the street from the hospital where she worked, was that I was able to change my insurance plan because it was open enrollment the very next day! This all happened without any effort. Something just changed.

When I met my new team, I felt a sense of calm. There was a complete shift.

Trust your gut. It will never, ever lead you wrong. Especially now. Speak up. If you are not completely in sync with your team, get a second opinion. It was the best decision I made during this journey.

Chapter Four:
The Love Shift

When Souls Connect

When I received my diagnosis, it was just a few weeks shy of my 22nd wedding anniversary. How could a love story like ours end up here? How had we drifted so far from each other? We had been in what felt like a standoff for the past three years. The fighting was so frequent and would escalate so fast we were feeding off each other in the worst way. This had been especially intense in the two months leading up to my diagnosis. I had reached a point of sheer exhaustion, and some days I no longer wanted to try to fix it. Where was the man I fell in love with? Where was I in this marriage? Where was he? It was such a far place from where we began, I couldn't believe we were at this place. I always felt we were so connected on a soul level. I was confused and scared, thinking our relationship was so fragile, how were we going to get through this together? I needed him more than ever, but this time I had to trust and let go, which was a very difficult process for me. But step by step, it happened.

In 1997, I was a single girl working in a sales job that I loved and living life on my own terms. I had had my heart broken and had made a conscious decision to be single. Inside though, I was ready to meet my partner, but I had put that aside and was just focused on my work and my friendships. Then out of the blue, a coworker of mine had just come from her dental checkup, and she was absolutely sure that I should meet the nice young dentist who had just taken over for her dentist that was retiring. I immediately thought this was a terrible idea, even making a snarky comment like, "Just because you are married doesn't mean that marriage is for everyone." I remember her just giving me a reassuring smile and walking away. Well, six months later, after her next dental checkup, she brought it up again. This time I didn't respond, but she had already put things into motion. She decided to take a chance and give him my number without asking me.

I answered the phone at my desk and heard this soft-spoken man's voice on the other end. He introduced himself as "Bill" and told me how he came to have my number and asked if I would like to meet for dinner. I was still stuck on what kind of Greek name 'Bill" was, so I asked him what his real name was? I could hear that he was smiling on the other side of the phone. I thought, Good, he gets me. That was my very first feeling about him. He explained that 'Bill" was his nickname. Since that phone call in December 1997, I have called him by his real name. We spoke for a few minutes and decided to have dinner the day after Christmas. December 26th, 1997.

I was nervous. This was very unusual for me. I had been on many dates but always felt in control. At this point, I was relying just on my instinct. If I was on a date with someone and I knew that we were not a match, I didn't pretend. I was straight forward and very matter-of-fact about the whole thing. Something about this particular date was different. I had even gone to Nieman's to buy a new dress and shoes. I had never done that before. He picked me up at my apartment. Once I saw him and he smiled, I fell in love at that moment. We were a natural fit from the beginning, complete opposites, but deeply connected on a soul level.

That first date lead to a date the next day and the next day and every day after that. We were engaged on February 1, 1998, just 38 days after we met. We had no plan—he was just starting out in his career, but we took a leap of faith, joined together, and built a life.

This romantic love story of ours was short-lived and so far away from the reality that we were living now. Something inside of me was hopeful we could find our way back to what brought us together so many years ago. I prayed about this all the time, asking for help. As I started to accept what was and forgive myself and my husband for all the pain that we had caused each other, things started to get better.

Our Song

My prayers were answered. I believe God had his hand in this because there were so many miracles that happened to help keep us together during this time. It all started with a song.

On Saturday night, we were scheduled to attend a wedding. At our phase of life, there weren't many weddings that we were invited to, so this was very unusual. I was a mix of emotions that day, like I was most days. One minute I felt great, and the next I felt as if my life was ending. Not what you would imagine as a great state of mind to be a wedding guest. I somehow managed to get myself together enough to go. We didn't know many people at the reception, so the two of us only had each other. That night, we briefly started to fall back into the natural rhythm that had brought us together in the first place. He was looking at me as if he was seeing me for the first time, and maybe he was—I was a completely different person now.

The wedding was beautiful and had divine timing for us. As couples danced and laughed all around us, I was hopeful that one day we could be a couple like that. And just as I had that thought, I heard a song come on and I could feel the vibration of energy send shivers up my spine. It was our wedding song ....I know this sounds fairly obvious that popular wedding songs would be playing at a wedding. However, our wedding song was not at all popular, and we had never heard it played at any wedding we had been to in the 22 years since our wedding. We both looked at each other in disbelief.

Tears welled up in my eyes and I looked at him and we both knew that something special had just happened. This was a clear sign.

My husband asked me to dance that night. We hadn't danced together since our wedding day. As we walked onto the dance floor and started to dance, it felt as if no time had gone by. All of the hardships and stresses of our marriage disappeared for those few minutes, and time stood still. I could no longer hear the music or see anyone else around us. Like I had lost my hearing and my sight, and all I could do is feel. I fell into his arms and rested my cheek on his shoulder. My body felt like Jell-O, and I wasn't able to move my legs, but somehow, they moved. A single tear fell down my cheek and onto his suit jacket. Everything was in slow motion. I felt safe, I felt loved. He was trying, and this glimpse of love started to help me come back to life. This was God, there was no doubt in my mind.

In order for us to get out of the dark place we were in, there had to be light. That night, I felt the light, even just for those few minutes on the dance floor. The connection that we had was always there; it was just buried under years of ego and blame. His eyes were looking right into my soul. I could feel how much he loved me. It was something I had needed for so long. Sometimes you need to go back to where you came from, the beginning. We had forgotten how to love each other. That night, everything changed for us. It was the first night of our new story. This story was full of hope and possibility. Thank God.

Memories of New York

Throughout this ten-week journey, we did things together that were new. One of the most incredible things we did was take trips to New York to see Apollonia. We hadn't been to New York together in over a decade. I would go often with friends or our girls, but we never went together, which is ironic because it's where we went on our second date the very next day after our first date.

I remember how incredible our very first trip was to New York almost 22 years ago. On the night of our first date in Boston, we were having so much fun; then at the end of the night, totally randomly, he asked me if I liked Indian food? I giggled and thought what a strange way to end a first date, and then answered honestly that no, I didn't. I already felt very comfortable around him even though we had just met a few hours before. He smiled with his quiet, confident smile and asked me for the opportunity to change my mind. "Be ready at nine o'clock tomorrow morning. I will pick you up then." This was so intriguing—who goes out for Indian food so early in the morning? I was so shocked that I accepted.

The next day was a Saturday; I had a standing hair appointment every Saturday—this is something that still happens to this day! I am very serious about my hair, and nothing up until that point in my 25-year-old life had ever come between me and my hairdresser. So you can imagine the utter shock when I called to cancel my appointment for a date with a guy I had just met. This was way out of character for me, but my instinct had taken over, and I just went with it.

I was ready to be picked up on this cold crisp December day. He pulled up right on time, and I could feel the sense of excitement between us. Here I was, in a car with a complete stranger, no idea where we were going, but I knew I was with my person. When we pulled onto Interstate 93 and took the exit to Logan airport, I looked over at him, confused. Where was he taking me—to eat at the airport? He could sense my confusion. "I'm taking you to New York to my favorite Indian restaurant and I think you will really like it. It's a very special place." My smile was so big; I still remember what my face felt like that day.

We spent a magical day in New York. The restaurant overlooked Central Park and was draped in beautiful Indian cloths from the ceiling to the floor. There were bright, colorful cushions on the floor to sit on instead of chairs. It was like nothing I had ever seen before. So bright and happy with an incredible view overlooking the park. It felt like we were in a movie. The conversation was easy, and we were so connected. Lunch went on for hours. He was so excited to share his love of Indian food with me. I didn't love it just yet, but I was on my way, for sure.

As the day turned into night, we found our way to a small cozy cafe in SOHO and sat there talking for hours. When we walked outside, it had just started snowing. In the light of the streetlamp, the snowflakes looked like diamonds falling softly from the sky. It was magical. We kissed, and I knew this was my person.

As I write about our love story, I still glow from the inside out. It was out of this world, better than anything

I could have ever dreamed of or prayed for. So how did we get to a place where we were so broken? The truth is, I think it was a series of things, and we lost each other in the process. I had tried for years to keep us together, but he had checked out of our relationship almost immediately after we got married. We both didn't realize this until the cancer. It suddenly had become so clear to both of us.

It started out small, little things here and there. Our personalities are very opposite. I am loud and outspoken, and he is quiet and methodical. In the early years of our marriage, we struggled to find a balance between the two. All I had ever known was to fight. I had lived my entire life always in survival mode. Just getting by and making everything look like it was okay on the outside. He also came with his deep, unresolved issues; however, he internalized them. He never spoke about anything that was bothering him. This was not a good combination.

I think this drove us apart. About four years into our marriage, our first daughter, Melina, was born. When that happened, our life and marriage changed completely. Now our focus was on someone else, and a couple of years later, Thalia was born. Our daughters became the focus of my life. I was so grateful that we became parents, especially to such incredible girls. There were happy years for some time. Our underlying issues as a couple were still there in the background, but with such busy lives with two small children and jobs, we pushed it down further and further. The main issue would come up in different ways over the years. Our marriage lacked physical intimacy, and that was a silent pain that I lived with. This would lead to so many fights and so much turmoil between us. I felt very alone and unloved in our marriage.

This was a burden I carried silently for many years. I struggled to even accept it myself, so it was hard for me to talk about it. I was frustrated and angry, and that came out in so many bad ways. My temper was volatile. No matter what we were fighting about—finances or what was best for our family—the argument would always end there. So the pattern for many years was I would yell, he would completely shut down, we would resolve nothing, and then we'd both be drained. He also wasn't willing to talk to anyone about these issues, and I resented him for this.

We grew further and further apart. He was solely focused on his work, and my focus was on the girls. It felt like we were on opposite sides of the world. And many times, we were. I would take the girls, and we would travel without him. His work was always his priority. We slipped into these roles, and along the way, we lost each other.

This was a horrible way to live. Both of us were so disconnected. Things would get better for a while, a few months at a time; then it would start all over again. This went on for many years throughout our marriage. As the girls got older and less dependent on us, we found ourselves in the worst place we had ever been. All the years of struggle had beaten us both down. What little patience I had left was now gone.

The warrior in me did all I knew how to do to keep my marriage together, but I had gone as far as I could go. I was tired. Ready to give up, we spoke that summer before my diagnosis about separating. This was the hardest time for me in our 22-year relationship. I had become indifferent. I stopped pretending that everything in my marriage and life was perfect. When I attended events alone, I didn't make excuses or try to cover up why he wasn't with me. As independent as I was, I was still so sad inside to always be alone.

We had put each other through so much pain; there were moments I felt that it was hopeless.

Yet we never left each other. I do believe that was God's work. Even when things got really bad between us, I never left, and neither did he. There must be a reason, I thought. Well, now the reason is clear to me.

We still had love for each other. I am not sure it was husband-and-wife love, but it was love.

During the ten weeks, we started slowly to come back to each other. This was the first of many miracles that happened over those ten weeks. I am grateful for each and every one. He and I went to New York multiple times over the next few weeks. We had so many incredible things happen for us during these visits.

The first time we went was September 28th. This time, instead of flying, we decided to drive. It was a beautiful fall day; the leaves had started turning pretty fall colors. The road was easy and wide open, just as it would be each time I traveled to New York to visit Apollonia. As we approached her apartment, I would immediately relax. Anytime that I could feel a release like that was like a little nudge from God for me to keep going.

We climbed the four flights of stairs to her apartment with me leading the way. The door was left open, and the super-bright sunshine had spilled out into the hallway. It felt like walking into heaven. Sitting at the table together, Apollonia looked at my husband, and with her kind, thoughtful eyes, she started to speak with him. Her voice was soft and kind, like an angel's whisper. "What has changed for you since this news about Joanna's health?"

He paused like I had seen him do countless times before, but then his eyes locked with mine. His eyes looked different; he looked present in that moment. Not distracted. This was a big change. One of the biggest challenges we had in our relationship was communication. When I had spoken to him over the past, he always seemed "not there." Completely checked out. Not this day; at this moment, he was right there. He then slowly moved his eyes to look at Apollonia and quietly replied, "Everything has changed. Now I have a sense of urgency, that time matters." It was as if now he realized that he had the possibility of losing me. This brought up a lot of emotions for me. Some good, some sad.

We sat at the table quietly for a few minutes. His answer was so pure and simple, just like our love when we first met. I felt love for him.

Reflections on Healing

Clearing Resistance

What is resistance? Resistance can show up in various forms and stop you in your tracks. It's the feeling that you don't like what 's going on, and you want it to change. So, you spend time creating a story in your mind about how things should be or how you wished they were. This creates resistance to what is actually going on and will add more stress to an already stressful situation.

There are many ways to look at this, but the reality is you have cancer and you are told to "fight it" or "beat it"— these are just well-meaning words that are floating out there all around us. I don't know about you, but I was scared and tired of "fighting." I felt like I had been in fight or flight for years before this—I was tired. It just doesn't make much sense to me to "go to war" at a time like this. War causes stress, strife, pain, and the list goes on and on.

This can be a challenging thing to grasp at first. Think about it. The goal here is for you to have the best possible experience with the least amount of stress. This situation is already stressful enough, and now you have to fight? Doesn't make much sense when you think about it that way, does it?

The great news is here everyone is looking for the same outcome. You, and all the people and messaging that are directing you to war. So how about you just simply shift the words in your mind? No need to share or explain to people because this can cause a debate, which is the very last thing you need at this moment. Instead, think differently for yourself. To those around you that are closest and who you know won't give you a hard time, ask them to change the words they use. Instead of "fight "and "beat," replace those words with "heal" and "healthy."

Even looking at those words, you cannot have the word "HEALTHY" if you don't first have "HEAL." Having people around you who are telling you that you are going to heal will put you in a much better mindset than hearing you going to have to fight; it's just a nicer feeling. Change the words and you help change the story.

What you resist persists—the thoughts you choose to verbalize are super important, especially here. "All is well."

Being Aware of Triggers

You can wake up in the morning feeling "good," and then one little thing can set you down a whole different path, and then the resistance will pop up. These days, anything can be a trigger. You could be watching a movie or show, and then one of the characters gets diagnosed with breast cancer, and this feels like someone punched you in the gut. You go to the grocery store, and as you are waiting in the checkout line, a magazine has "breast cancer" written on the front cover. You are watching TV, and every other commercial is about a drug that's either related to cancer or it's a drug that one of its side effects could possibly cause breast cancer. It's like a minefield.

This can set you on the path of resistance in seconds. Your intentions here, paired with verbal action, can release you from this. Think of it as a workout routine that helps you build the muscles that can "pick up" the resistance and throw it in the trash.

Two-Step Process

This is a simple two-step process—it has to be because you will want to make this a habit.

Intend and Verbalize—thinking of this as a "catch and release."

When the resistance comes up and that feeling takes over your whole body, you can feel paralyzed. This is where you put your catch and release into action. Step one, the "catch" is to be aware—just know it's happening. This is the "intended awareness." You know it's happening, and you don't suppress it or push it down. Instead, do the opposite. Acknowledge it—like, I see you and I know you're here. Bringing this awareness with deliberate intention to release it will help stop it from growing. Then right away, put words to it. And at the end of those words, add "all is well." Keep it simple and say it out loud. Yup, that's right, no matter what or how bad it is, finish what you are saying with "all is well."

This is something I learned by listening to Joel Osteen. As I was looking at how best I could help you get through this, I was struggling to put it into words. So I took a break and read a passage from one of his books, and it was right in front of me. It was so obvious, and I wished I had used it at the end of every single sentence that came out of my mouth during my ten weeks in the "waiting room." It's easy and simple and free and available to all of us. Take advantage of adding those words to the end of what you say when you feel resistance come up.

Here is an example: You get a call from your doctor, saying that the second spot that they found in the MRI also tested positive for cancer. This will most likely set you on the path of resistance. Thoughts can come flooding into your mind like, "Oh no, it's spread!" or "Now I might have to take a different course of action." Although these things are extremely real, be aware that it's your own story that you are creating about what "could happen" that is causing resistance at that exact moment.

This is how you can choose to apply this technique to help you at a time like this. Bring intended awareness to it by accepting whatever the information is. This is important: I don't want you to ignore or pretend this isn't happening—that will only cause bigger issues. Call it like you see it. Like, "Oh shit, my doctor called and the second spot is cancer that sucks. It's not the news I wanted or hoped for." You have acknowledged the facts but haven't added a future story to the facts that will cause you to build resistance. This is the intended awareness part. Then, how you frame it verbally actually gives it life. This is the second part of working through resistance. You repeat out loud, "Oh shit, my doctor called and the second spot is cancer that sucks. It's not the news I wanted or hoped for, BUT ALL IS WELL."

This will feel strange in the beginning, or even every time you do it, but it works. It releases the resistance to what is actually happening. That's okay, keep going—one foot in front of the other, just keep going. That's all you need to do here.

Once you develop this muscle, it will spill over into every part of your life. It can even change the lenses in which you view your entire life.

Learning to Accept

The only way to work through resistance is acceptance. That sounds so simple, yet it can be one of the hardest things to do. At least it was for me.

It will keep creeping up. Resistance can show up disguised as many things. Be aware of who and what you are listening to. This is extremely important because even well-meaning people who love you can trigger resistance in you. Limit your exposure to stories that people want to share that might make you scared.

Have an exit strategy for when you're on the phone with people or in in-person situations like this. Here are a few that worked for me:

- I have to jump on a call with the girls' school. Let's talk another time.
- Oh no, I forgot that my mom called and I have to call her back. Let's talk another time.
- I just realized I am late for a conference call, sorry.
- Oh, that's my doctor calling on another line. Got to go.

- My neighbor just stopped by. Let's talk later.

If you are in an in-person situation, here are a few ways to get through:

- Try to get up and go to the bathroom whenever possible. Look in the mirror at yourself and tell yourself, "All is well."
- Be honest and say that you don't feel like talking about this right now and excuse yourself.
- Look at your phone and have a few pictures on hand that make you instantly feel better. Focus on those.
- If possible, go outside and take a deep breath.
- Leave if you can. There is nothing wrong with leaving, and don't overexplain.

How to Accept Love

This was the hardest one for me. Period. Even though I knew how to give love, I really sucked at accepting it. It's something I still work on daily. I had built up a nice facade over the course of my life. A personality is really a great cover for this—mine was. Because I am so outgoing and friendly, it was easy to mask.

I had put up these protective walls to make sure I was never hurt or abandoned again. This had taken such a toll on me inside. Well, there is nothing like a cancer diagnosis to get you to change. This is the time. Let go today of the expectations you have of how others should love you.

The biggest cover-up in my life was my marriage. I had been deeply unhappy for at least a decade. I worked hard to hide this and to keep my family together. Putting my best foot forward to make it look to others and to myself and our daughters that everything was okay. I always knew deep down that it wasn't. My husband, who is a very kind and nice person, was never a partner in our marriage. He never participated on a basic level in our marriage. We lived very separate lives in the same household for most of our marriage. I put everything I had into our children and maintaining relationships with both our families and all our friends. I tried my hardest to make it all okay, or at least appear that way. He put all his efforts into his work and had no interest in us. This caused so much anger and resentment in me, and it created a turbulent relationship that was exhausting on a daily basis. However, we had stayed together, and now this ….

I say this because it's a miracle that I was still married at the time of my diagnosis. So, I understand firsthand how hard this can be. Your instinct might be that this is the time to close off any relationships that have brought you pain or difficulty. I understand. This is the time to accept them as they are. I am not by any means suggesting you accept someone who is treating you poorly. I am suggesting that for now, until you heal, park that relationship in a parking lot and leave it there.

Your instinct might be that you want more than ever to leave, but this might not be the right time. Instead, make a list on paper for yourself with all of the things that you are going to do to keep yourself well in that situation, regardless of what the other person is doing. You know deep down what the issues are. I am not suggesting you ignore them; I am saying park them for right now. Make a conscious decision to just accept what is without infusing it with what you hoped it would be. This is YOUR time—whatever relationship(s) have drained you before this, don't give them your energy now. You need all your energy to get well and heal. This is the first step to self-love. With this, you will begin to learn how to accept love.

Don't be afraid; I know it can feel scary. If you are in a safe situation, accept that you are staying in it, for now at least. Leaving will just add gasoline to the fire. There is freedom in having no expectations from the other person, accepting them how they are. This is not forever; it's just for now. When you are healed, you will have more information and can make any changes you wish then.

This is how you can open yourself up: Start each morning with a clear intention for yourself to accept love. A simple way to do this is when you are washing your hands after you first go to the bathroom in the morning. Look in the mirror, smile at yourself, and say I love you! This will probably feel awkward in the beginning, but it's easy, free, and you are not doing anything else at the time when you are washing your hands after using the toilet, so why not love yourself?

Once you get comfortable doing that in the morning, add it in throughout the day. If you are anything like me and you pee 1,000 times per day, well, that's a lot of I love you's!!! You can't hear it enough. It's awesome and will make you feel better right away. If you are in your bathroom at work or in a public restroom, and you are worried that people will think you lost your shit—I get it—here is a modification: Look yourself in the eyes, smile, and see how many times you can silently say I love you while washing your hands.

If you are a mom and you never ever are in the bathroom alone, this can be an awesome teaching experience. You are saying I love you to yourself in front of your kids. I can't think of a better behavior they could model.

If you have teenagers who barge into your bathroom to ask you if they can buy something online or to raid your high-end beauty creams, they will think you have gone completely crazy. Who cares? Hopefully, it will seep into their partially developed brain as well. All we can do is try, right?

This gives a whole new meaning to "mirror selfie"— Who cares? Injecting a love exercise into something you already do without adding additional work for yourself is a no-brainer. This works, and it makes you feel good, so do it. This will open up the love to flow from others.

You must let go of what you think love should look like. We all have these stories in our heads about what it should be like, and when it's not what we imagined or hoped, we resist it. Let that shit go. It hasn't served you, so it's time to try a new way. This is a tough one for me. But if I can do it, so can you.

This is not to be confused with letting people treat you badly or take advantage of your kindness. It just means don't create a story in your head to make a situation worse. Here is a real-life example:

You get a call from your doctor and you are so upset and scared. Then you try to carry on with your day. Then you get a call with one of your relationships that is challenging. Could be your spouse or your mother. They say or do something that bothers you. You get upset. Then you take the story further in your head: "They don't love me, or I don't deserve that, or They are so mean. Any of these could actually be true—my question to you is this: Does that help you feel better right now? NO, it doesn't. So a way to deal with it is to say out loud, "I accept that is how they are." Chances are they are not going to miraculously change now. in fact, this can sometimes heighten and bring out more challenging parts of the relationships that were previously strained.

I came to terms with this during this "waiting room time" by saying, "If they knew better, they would do better." I was listening to a podcast from Oprah and Elkhart Tolle explaining his book *A New Earth*. Although I had listened to it at the beginning of the year, I went back to that episode where they were explaining that if people knew better, they would do better. This helped remind me that everyone is really doing the best they can. Even if their best is not up to your expectations, it's still their best. I also remember her saying that now that she knows better, she does better.

I am here to remind you that you know better, so do better for yourself. Stop fighting to change someone; they won't change. So accept them for who they are and whatever form of love they can offer you. Take it—it will either grow from there or fizzle out. Either way, it's better than the mental ping-pong you may have been playing all these years. The truth is, you are never unhappy because of another person; you are only disappointed in them, and that causes you to be unhappy. Accepting them and their love as it is will make your time in the "waiting room" much more bearable.

Just to be completely clear, you are doing this for yourself—just for YOU.

Accepting love is crucial to your healing. How you do it is up to you; these are just a few ways you can break the toxic cycle you may be living in. Take what works for you and just try. Try for you. You are worth it; you deserve it. You are going through enough, don't let anyone else take up real estate in your mind with issues that have been around forever. This time is YOUR time for love, and it starts by loving yourself.

Make a commitment that every time you wash our hands and there is a mirror, you'll look at yourself and say, "I love you." This simple shift will change your life.

...

Chapter Five:
The Renewal
of Faith

God Is on the Line

It was a perfect New York fall morning. After a healing session with Apollonia the day before, we went out to a fabulous dinner at the Polo Bar. I had always wanted to go there, and although it was very difficult to get a reservation, the incredible and kind concierge Krista at the St. Regis Hotel somehow made it happen. She later told me that she could tell by my voice that I was going through something and really wanted to help me. In fact, there were so many "moments of favor" just like that on this journey. Things that just seemed to work out for no reason and without effort. Like we would check into our hotel and the concierge would upgrade us to an imperial suite, even though we had reserved the most basic room using points. Strangers I had never met would offer to help me or make something better, out of the blue. The energy around me had shifted, and it became very obvious I was heading toward a better life.

On that Sunday morning, I noticed a church that I had walked by countless times in the past and had never really given it any attention. It was across the street from our hotel. I felt so drawn to this church but had no idea why. I had never gone into a church before, completely alone. This wasn't a Greek church, a Catholic church or a Jewish temple, all of which I was familiar with. This was new and different.

I sat in a pew quietly and waited with anticipation for the pastor to speak. The church was packed, but I felt as if he was speaking only to me. Then I hear the two words that made everything clear … Kyrie Eleyison. What a coincidence that it is Greek for "Lord, have mercy." The entire service was based on those two words. I grew up hearing these words weekly at church as it is a response in the Greek Orthodox service. How incredible that at this church, on that particular day, this was the service. It was new and familiar at the same time. Exactly what I needed.

If my faith was so deep and clear, then how come I was still scared? I was petrified. All these wonderful gifts and signs of faith were happening daily, and some days I was so overtaken by fear that I couldn't even see them. I would become paralyzed and go to this unimaginably dark place in my mind. My mind then would overtake my body, and I would feel physically unwell. Drained and exhausted. This cycle would last for a few hours to sometimes days. Where was God?

This was something I struggled with throughout. I need to jump ahead in the story here because it wasn't until well after my surgery that I had really answered this question for myself.

At this point, I was stuck in my writing of this book. I felt like a fraud. Like someone who had a deep faith, and yet I was still scared and asking God why—this felt like a contradiction. How could I be writing about all of the wonderful things that have happened and had gone my way and yet still be filled with fear, anxiety, and questioning God?

I decided to close my computer and go take a yoga class across the street at the Equinox fitness club. It was about three months since my surgery, and the doctors had given me the all clear to return to exercise. Working out had become such a huge part of my life over the past 17 years, yet when the doctor said I could go back, I didn't want to. I was scared. My body craved the physical activity, but socially I was having a hard time. My surgery was a huge success, and I am cancer-free, but the thought of facing people I hadn't seen in months and answering questions about how I was doing overwhelmed me. It felt like each time I was reliving it over and over. People are so caring and kind and well-meaning, and for that I am grateful, but this part was really hard.

Something that day just felt right, and I decided to go for it, thanks to a dear friend who had encouraged me to meet her at a class a few days before and had helped me with my "reentry." It felt like a minefield, each familiar face I saw eager to ask me how I was. I am a very social and outgoing person, but now I crave quiet. Like anything you do for the first time since surgery, it feels different now. Not better or worse, just different.

I walked into the class and placed my mat toward the back of the room. This was new for me. I was always the front and center kind of girl. This was a humbling experience, for sure. I did it anyway. When I started to practice yoga years ago, I almost walked out of the studio on the first day because I was so intimidated. This felt like I was starting over. I was in many ways.

I was struggling that day to find my new rhythm. Going back to doing things I used to do before. It's like everything and everyone around me stayed the same, and yet I was completely different.

That day in yoga, I got the answer I was looking for. It was Valentine's Day, and the instructor started telling a story about what true love was. She talked about how the night before she had been up all night with her young son who was sick, and that that was true love. Then she added that her son had asked her in the middle of the night why God was doing this to him. I froze when I heard this. Throughout this journey, I had never wondered why God was doing this to me because I never believed he was. So I thought about this little boy and how I would have answered him or my own daughters if they had asked. God wasn't doing this to you, but God sees everything, and it will all be okay. And there, on my yoga mat, I found the answer I was searching for.

I had to remind myself that he always sees, and he knows what I am going through.

I had always prayed and had an open dialog with God. In fact, I don't ever remember not talking to God.

God is good all the time. So why did I experience fear? I felt very connected to my faith, yet my mind would hijack me, and I would go into this dark place full of fear and anxiety.

I knew that in order for me to continue healing, I would have to really feel what I was talking about. I would really have to connect with myself and God.

Everything Is Under Control

Can you have faith and still feel fear? I say, yes. This goes back to my internal struggle, like two sides of me inside fighting against each other. I did a great job outwardly practicing staying in faith, but inside the conversation seemed different. I could be in church experiencing a moment of peace, and then as I walked to my car immediately after the service, I would be paralyzed by fear and anxiety.

These episodes would come on so fast, and I felt like someone had stepped into my physical body and taken over. Here I was doing all the "right things": eating a healthy diet, exercising, being a meditator, a yogi, a follower of God, and this still happened to me. I believe, for me, it was my internal struggle that I worked so hard to hide that was the catalyst.

I had to surrender and accept myself exactly where I was in order to realign with God. Forgive myself for past mistakes. There was always a dark, internal undertone; a voice that spoke to me to tell me what I had done was so terrible, that I wasn't enough and that I wasn't worthy of a life filled with love. I worked so hard to hide this from everyone. God had other plans for me. Nothing like facing your own mortality to give you a swift kick in the ass.

I needed change, and I needed it now. The change came. With one phone call, my life had moved into two different parts: life before cancer and life after cancer. God must have seen all the parts of me that needed to heal.

I was seeing signs each day, even on the hardest days. Not as if any of the days were easy, but some were worse than others. My faith always brought me out of it. On October 1st, I woke up and felt such sadness. The weekend was over. We were back from an incredible trip to NYC to see Apollonia. Now it was Monday; my husband was off to work, my girls were at school, and I was left with lots of time to think. I would think for a few minutes about the good outcomes, then my mind would go right back to the dark side. Hours would pass like this. On that morning, I was struggling to even get out of bed when I received a text message from Christen. It was a screenshot saying: Good Morning, I have everything under control, God. I felt an instant surge of hope. I had probably seen that message scrolling on Instagram before, but today it felt as if God himself had texted it to me. It worked; I got out of bed. That was a step. The week ahead was a tough one. I prayed and asked for help to get me through; for something more than I was already doing that could help me.

The answer came after my meditation that morning. I set up a large group text, which I used as a form of one-way communication with all my extended family and friends. This gave me something that I could do for myself. I am so blessed with so many people who love and care about me, but I was overwhelmed with the communication. My ability to answer any questions at all was overwhelming to me. So setting up this way of communication alleviated that stress, for the most part.

I put together a message explaining that I was so grateful for all the love and support and that I needed prayers. I also explained that I couldn't answer any questions because I was going to focus 100% on my healing. I would use this group to update my loved ones with real-time information and updates without having to reply to each person individually, and for me, most importantly, without having to answer any questions. I'm not sure why the questions drove me as crazy as they did, they actually still do, but I have gotten better at my reaction (at least I think I have). People mean so well, and it comes from such a deep love and caring, but I just couldn't engage.

My phone had become a minefield; each time it rang, it felt like I was getting punched in the gut. This feeling would remain throughout the ten weeks and beyond after my surgery while I was waiting for all my pathology results. That meant every telemarketer call was answered—I think that was just as brutal as the diagnosis! There should be a law making all sales calls during that time illegal to give people waiting for calls from their doctors less stress. Just saying,

Setting up that group text was one of the best decisions I made during that time, and I recommend it to anyone going through something like this. It gave me back a sense of control. Instead of having to communicate about this throughout the day, this made it simple, and I didn't have to think of it each time I looked at my phone. It was a simple, free solution that made my life so much better.

I hope that it was helpful to my friends and family. I know how hard it is when someone you love is going through something like this. You are not sure what to say, how you can help etc. You want the person to know you care and that you love them, so you call, text, and offer help. It's so nice, and I have done it for many myself. The questions that people would ask me were the hardest part, mostly because I was scared of the answers myself. I didn't know what the plan was going forward for surgery, and I didn't know what, if anything, would be needed beyond that.

Each time someone would ask me, I would get so upset. I knew they meant well, but I could sense their own stress and fear when they asked, which made me even more scared. I prayed about this and how to handle it without becoming a complete crazy bitch to the people I love. Not sure if the mission was accomplished or not, but by setting up that text, it gave me the space I needed to be with my own fear and not take on other people's fears for me.

I had a lot to think about during this waiting period, a lot to contemplate. I fell back into my old patterns so many times, of getting angry and losing my temper. Each time that would happen, I felt like I was being overtaken by something foreign. This behavior no longer fit with who I was becoming. It drained me so fast that it would take me a few days to fully recover. I knew there was no way I could hold on to these old patterns and heal. No matter how amazing the doctors were or how effective the medicine is, I had to give up what no longer served me and help myself.

I had read so many books over the years that would help me do this. *The Secret, A New Earth, The Seat of the Soul, The Untethered Soul, The Four Agreements, The Seven Spiritual Laws, Return to Love, The Power of Now, Super Attractor, The Book of Joy.* These books, all so beautiful and filled with their own unique messages, at their core, had similarities: God was the common denominator.

I am grateful to have read these incredible books, some of them multiple times. Now I had to put into action what I had read over the years. To release my fear and doubts, and through acceptance, allow love into my heart. To receive love.

God was with me every step of this journey. Even in my darkest moments. God was there. That's true love.

Reflections on Healing

Aligning with Your Soul

GRATITUDE, PRAYER, MEDITATION, FAITH:
"The Fab Four"

Unpack your bag—you are moving into this new space in your life.

This is the fun part of this unfun process. I believe that these four things in any form can help you in any crisis, but especially now. Do all four or start with one, whatever works for you. But what if you are like me and you were already doing these things and this happened to you anyway? Well, that was the million-dollar question I had. I guess I was looking at it the wrong way before I had cancer. Like, I do all the "right" things, or I am trying so hard. Even though I was doing these things, some of them my entire life, there was still one major thing missing— I hadn't unpacked my bag.

In order to truly heal from any disease, I believe that you need to be at peace with yourself and your past. This sounds like something we have all read before. I know, believe me, I wanted it so badly to be at peace; to really just let it all go. But I couldn't hold on for the long term. The traumas of my past would always creep up and pull me back. So, I am the first to admit that although I was doing these four things, I was still not aligned. Stay with me here—learn from my mistakes. The talk that was going on in my head would take over, and I felt defeated.

Making this one simple change in your vocabulary will open up the space to set you on the course of alignment: remove the word "but." Yes, start there. Stop using it—it's what is keeping your bag packed and stuck in your past.

It has never been more important for you to be in the present moment. If not now, when? I had the most incredible surgeons and doctors working to remove my cancer, however, I knew if I didn't change my old patterns, I would never truly be healed. I felt with every cell of my body that in order for my surgery to work, I had to align my soul with my physical body. Which, to me, meant getting my inside to match my outside.

For years, I had hidden behind my physical appearance. Making things look better than they really were. Wearing it like a mask. Hiding pain from my childhood, the loss of my father, things I had done as an adolescent, and my marriage. This bag that I was carrying around was so heavy, and now I knew that the cancer didn't fit into this bag. It was time to unpack.

I went through this process during the ten weeks I had between the phone call telling me I had cancer to the time I was on the surgical table. I asked for forgiveness from others and myself. I got very honest about my life and what I was always feeling inside. This would prove to be a very good start to my unpacking. When I started writing this book, my intention was to help you fully "unpack" your bag so you could have the best possible hope to heal from your cancer. As I reflect back, I realize that was very naive of me. The truth is, I am still working on it myself. It's like throwing away your old comfy sweatshirt because it was just time; it had so many holes you could no longer wash it. You know it had to be done, and it was time, but on some days, you'll still miss it. That's okay—but it was time for it to go.

You may have more than one sweatshirt that you need to "unpack." Be kind to yourself and start with one. Start with truly forgiving yourself and others, no matter what. Slowly, you will see that that the dingy sweatshirts full of holes that you couldn't imagine living without have been replaced with beautiful sweaters that are bright and look so good on you.

I found the four things that I was doing all along worked once I got honest with myself. Once I "unpacked." Start unpacking and incorporate one or all of these, and you will start to align. You will start having more good days and eventually return to your original self, the person you were always meant to be.

Chapter Six: Purgatory in Purgatory

Meditation and an MRI

It was nearly a month since the original phone call that changed my life. I am completely aware that when things are moving at a slower pace like this, it is a good thing in the sense that it is not an emergency. However, it still sucks. The waiting is the hardest part. I have heard it described as purgatory, and I would say that sums it up pretty well. Then there is the waiting within the waiting, which is even worse. Getting the call to say you have this is the first part, then more scans, and in my case, additional biopsies. Then you wait for those results. Brutal. For me, this was complete torture. Like it's not bad enough you have this inside of you, now you are wondering if there is more? I found this time to be the hardest.

I woke up early to meditate before my biopsy. I had been meditating for almost two years by this time. I don't think I could have made it through this whole experience without it. It was my go-to tool. I meditated each morning for 20 minutes, no matter what. The type of meditation that I practice, TM, is an individual mantra-based meditation that you practice twice a day for 20 minutes. It took the edge off, for sure. I think without this, I would have turned to alcohol to self soothe like I had done in the past whenever I had a stressful life situation.

Alcohol to cope was a part of my life before I had learned to meditate. I would use it to destress, sometimes a glass of wine, and sometimes a bottle. I had learned to use it as a release, especially when my children were younger. As soon as they would go to bed, I would pour myself a glass of wine to take away the stress of the day. This became a habit that went on for years. I had a love-hate relationship with it. I knew that sometimes I drank too much, and that made me feel terrible, emotionally and physically. I didn't like the way it made me feel, but I kept reaching for it whenever I had stress.

When I learned Transcendental Meditation, that went away. Without effort. I simply didn't think about it. I no longer reached for a glass of wine to help me "relax." This was such a gift. It allowed me to have a healthy relationship with alcohol. This is the first gift that TM gave me, but there are many others that helped me so much, especially going through this difficult time. It was a lifesaver, and I couldn't recommend it more. It made such a difference in my life that those who are closest to me also noticed a huge change and went and learned it themselves. In fact, after my surgery and my recovery, my husband saw how much this helped me and was so grateful that he went to learn himself. This was a huge step for him, as well as our relationship.

Having this tool allowed me to remain myself. I didn't need anything outside of me to "take the edge off." It's a game changer regardless of what's going on in your life. If you are reading this because you have been diagnosed with cancer, or any disease, this is something you can add to whatever you are already doing to bring you peace. If you are reading this because you are supporting a loved one going through something, this will give you the support you need to help them as well as yourself. If you are reading this because you work in healthcare, this will help you cope with all you see and hear each day. You can start wherever you are; just make sure you find an authorized teacher in your area, which you can do through the website. It's one of the best decisions I have ever made.

My husband took me to my biopsy that morning. Fresh from my meditation, I showered and put on my workout clothes. We left very early on that Wednesday morning for the hospital. I was especially grateful that he was taking me. It was rare for him to miss work at all, but almost never on a Wednesday. It was the busiest day of the week at one of his practices, but thankfully he was able to be there with me because this was hard.

It was October 2nd, and because October is Breast Cancer Awareness month, there were signs of pink everywhere. My radiologist, who was so kind and sweet, had even dyed his hair pink! The nurses and staff were like angels. The plan was to take another MRI and then biopsy the spots that they had identified a few weeks before to see if they were still there. I had been praying for the spots to be gone. That there would be no need for this. I went into the same room I had been in a few weeks ago. I was shaking. This time I couldn't have music, so I started to pray silently.

They took the images; the sound of the MRI machine was so loud. I was lying belly down with my breasts falling into the position where they would have to remain super still. The nurse was like an angel and had her hand on my back the whole time. She never left my side. She was so loving and kind and spoke to me the whole time. We realized that we had grown up in the same city, gone to the same high school (although she was much younger than me), and that she loved going to eat at my parents' restaurant. This was a gift from God—I don't think I could have gotten through this procedure without her.

Once the doctor took a look, he told me that one of the spots was gone. This was great news! However, the other spot that they had originally seen was still there, and they would have to move forward with a needle biopsy. He told me I had to remain completely still. With the nurse holding my back, I closed my eyes and surrendered to the process. I had no other choice. This was one of my many moments of surrender during this process. Once the procedure was over, the nurse whispered in my ear that I had done great and asked if I was a meditator? I smiled and nodded.

Getting through that procedure was hard. It was emotionally hard, and physically, it just put me in a funk. It felt barbaric to me. I knew now that I had to wait for the results, which was the absolute worst part. The waiting within the waiting.

Emotions All Over the Place

I went home, changed into my pajamas, and got into bed. I didn't feel like talking to anyone. This procedure had psychologically affected me. I felt vulnerable and violated. The time after the biopsy and waiting for the results were the most difficult days for me. Especially when I was expecting results on October 4th, my 21st wedding anniversary. So many emotions. My marriage was in such a vulnerable place before this even happened. Now we were trying to find a new way, closer to the way we were when we first fell in love. This was a process. Each day was different, some good, some not so good. I still had so much anger toward him. Even though I had my part in why we were where we were in our relationship, I mostly blamed him for not trying. I was vocal about how I felt. I wasn't one to hold back my feelings in the past, but now I was on a whole other level. I just wanted to make sure I was heard.

We were making steps in the right direction. I had committed to forgiving him for years of neglect. He had committed to forgiving me for my yelling and aggression. This was the first step. Before, each time we had tried to do this, it seemed that we were going in circles. We had tried before, but he had never committed like this. In the past, it was mostly me making the effort, and he would try for a few weeks and then give up. This would disappoint me, and I would get so angry, then sad. This was our old familiar pattern. By recognizing this and admitting that we both had a piece in this, not just him, we were able to start to break the cycle. This diagnosis served as a wakeup call for both of us, at least that is what I hoped.

This week was particularly filled with dark moments as I waited for the results of the needle biopsy. The day after the procedure was particularly hard, even though I knew I wouldn't receive a call with results, I was still sucker punched each time my phone rang. I stayed in bed most of the day feeling sorry for myself. I gave myself that one day to sulk and just be. I didn't talk to anyone. Although friends were reaching out, I just couldn't talk. I needed the day to myself for myself. Tomorrow would be better, I thought. I was hopeful that they would call with good results.

They never called …. This was the absolute hardest part. We had plans to attend a dear friend's party that evening. It was our anniversary, and I really wanted to go out and have fun, but I just couldn't. I couldn't handle small talk, had zero interest in what anyone had to say about anything and didn't want to talk about my situation. Not great party guest qualities. I was so drained; I just couldn't rally. I decided not to go. This is something I never would have done before, canceling at the last minute. Instead of doing what I would usually do—power through, go and put on a good show, and pretend that I was doing great—I did the opposite. I listened to what my soul needed.

This was a huge step in my healing journey. My pleasing nature and my ego had always won out in these cases. Not anymore. That night, as hard as it was, I learned that I had to give myself a break. That it's okay to not be okay. That it was okay to ask for help. That my friends would still love me anyway. That night, my husband and I went to dinner at our favorite neighborhood restaurant. It was exactly what I needed.

The next day was Saturday, and I had a ticket to go see Esther Hicks (a spiritual channel). I was a huge fan, yet that morning you would have thought that I was getting dragged to a torture chamber. I was in a bad place mentally. The dialogue in my mind had overtaken reality. I thought if I surrounded myself with high vibration people, maybe it would snap me out of it. So I got myself out of bed, put on a cute outfit and some makeup, and headed the 20 miles north to where the event was.

On my way, I got a text from a good friend. It was about a family situation she had and something we had talked about for years. We would always help each other out that way by talking things through. For some reason, this morning it set me into a complete spiral. I felt like what I was going through superseded everything. How could my friend even message me about something like this? I flipped out. I called her and went completely nuts. I had a complete meltdown; tears were flooding my face, and I was screaming on the phone. I let it all out. I told her that yesterday I had been waiting for results all day and I was alone. I had tried calling her and all of the friends in our friend group, but I couldn't reach anyone. She was blindsided. She had no idea. I had never asked anyone to be with me; I assumed they would just know what I needed.

Well, that was impossible because I didn't know what I needed, so how on earth could they know? I also told her that I didn't have the capacity to give advice about anything at the moment because everything else seemed so stupid. This was not my best friendship moment. I had never expressed my feelings that way to my friends before. I was honest and raw. It was a breakthrough. I am the luckiest girl in the world because of all the incredible friends I have. My friendships mean everything to me. I am so grateful that my friend responded with patience, love, and understanding that day.

I cleaned myself up as best I could in the car and then headed in to see Abraham channeled by Esther Hicks. I was feeling so sorry for myself and feeling bad for flipping out on my friend. I couldn't imagine a better time to change my frequency. When I walked into the large room and started looking for a chair, I gravitated to the back, which was not usual for me. I always liked to sit in the front of every room, except for church (sorry, Father). I found a chair in the back corner. I sat down, shoulders slumped and all. A woman tapped my shoulder to ask if anyone was sitting in the empty chair next to me. I nodded, signifying, no. I don't think I even looked up at her. The two of us sat quietly, waiting for Esther to come on stage.

She looked stressed and anxious like I was. I wondered if this woman has something similar to me going on. I introduced myself; she had kind eyes, and we started to talk. She shared with me that she was going through a difficult situation with her son, that he was a heroin addict, that she was raising her grandson and working hard to support her other children and grandson, all while worrying about her drug-addicted son.

Yup, turns out I wasn't the only one with a problem. This woman's pain and struggle were unimaginable to me. Then I thought about my friend who was dealing with what seemed to me like a "small" problem. I thought all of these are the same. My situation, my friends, and the woman I just met. Hurt is hurt, no matter what. This opened my eyes to look at things in a different way. There is no judgment about who is hurting more or whose problem is more important, etc. This was a great lesson for me. It doesn't mean that I immediately dove back into listening to friends complaining about stuff we all complain about, but I understood.

Realize that people's lives haven't changed, yours has. The things that they complained about before they will continue to complain about. It's okay. You can't expect everyone around you to change because you had a life-changing situation. Just be aware of how you feel. People are trying to help, but they don't know how. Be as clear as possible. It's okay to tell your friends that, for right now, you don't have the capacity to listen to everything. This is a hard shift for you and them, especially if you are the one that is always the "go-to" person. The "go-to" person is going in for service and will be out of commission until further notice.

The weekends were the hardest. This weekend especially because I hadn't received my results. The girls would be home, which you think would bring comfort, but it didn't. I love my girls more than life itself, but I just found it hard to be around them. This made me sad. I just didn't have the energy. I always had been the one to keep it all together. Making sure everyone had what they needed and could get to where they needed to be. This particular weekend I spent counting the hours until Monday when I thought I would get the biopsy results. Full of anxiety and stress. I could barely keep it together. My girls saw me be vulnerable and scared. This was freeing to my soul. I took a step back from "mom" mode and hoped my husband would step in. This was so good for the girls in so many ways. It showed them, for the first time, that he and I could work as a team. I was always hopeful that we could come together and function as a family unit, and this showed me it was possible.

The Power of Acceptance

Monday came and went without a phone call from my doctor. This was one of the hardest days of this ten-week journey. Of course, every telemarketer on the planet decided to call that day. Each time the phone rang, I felt like I was swallowing my heart. Brutal. By Tuesday morning, I was a complete train wreck. I couldn't take it one more day. I put a call in to my doctor, hoping to reach him as it was the start of the Jewish holiday, and I knew he would be observing. By the grace of God, he got my message, and even though he was off, he had the kindness to go to his office and get my pathology results. I was so grateful for this. I just couldn't handle the waiting any longer. He called, and the news wasn't what we had hoped. The needle biopsy confirmed that the second spot was also cancer. This felt like I was living the first call all over again.

Then suddenly, a feeling of peace and relief came over me. I caught my breath, and things appeared clearly to me for the first time since my diagnosis. I knew that removing that breast was going to be the best option, and if that was going to be the case, I would have both removed. I could put the stress and worry of 15 years about mammograms, ultrasound, and biopsies behind me. I had a path forward.

I called my husband to tell him the news. He was on his way home from work, and we made plans to meet for dinner so we wouldn't discuss this at home where the girls were just getting home from school. This felt similar to the first phone call: the voice of the doctor in slow motion, each syllable taking ten times longer than usual. But this time I felt stronger, not as blindsided. This information gave me a medical path forward. I was grateful to have a plan.

When I walked outside on that beautiful fall evening, the sky was lit up in bright pink. I had never seen the sky look like that before. It was the most breathtaking thing

I had ever seen. This was a sign just for me, I thought.
As I crossed my street, I heard my phone ping. I looked
down to see it was a message from a friend, a young girl
who had been going through treatment for cancer for
whom my family and I had done some fundraising. It was
the most incredible message. It said: I am cancer-free.
I burst into tears; I was so happy to hear good news.
This inspired me. She inspired me.

My husband and I had a nice dinner; it felt as if a
huge weight had been lifted. It was peaceful. I felt loved.
I had phoned Joy and Michaella to tell them the news.
They both came after dinner to meet me. When one of
them walked by outside the restaurant, she could see
my husband and me holding hands through the window. Once she mentioned it, I smiled. I hadn't realized
it, but we had been holding hands throughout most of
the night. We all sat for hours talking that night. It was
gentle and kind. I was surrounded by love. The love
of my husband, the love of my friends, the love of the
universe wrapping me up in that gorgeous pink sky. It
felt like I was in a good movie.

The next day, I woke up with a new sense of peace.
I had scheduled Apollonia to do a remote session with
me that day. It was exactly what I needed. On that day,
I started to surrender and find acceptance of what was
happening to my body. I was never in denial about what
was going on, but I was mad about it. That combination
caused friction and resistance. If I was going to really heal,
I had to start to let things go. I committed to releasing
my anger so I could truly accept what was happening.

Once I had made up my mind, even before talking to any of my doctors, this took a load off of me. The not knowing was the hardest part. I used this time for as much self-care as I could get and doing things that made me feel good.

I took Joy to lunch for her birthday. This is something we had done for years, and it felt good to do something I enjoyed that didn't involve me talking about my diagnosis. Although we did end up there after a bit of rosé, now that I had made my decision, it was easier.

I decided to go full throttle into my spiritual side. All in. I put everything I had on the table and surrendered. Over the course of the next few weeks, there were so many signs and moments that kept me going. I put all of my energy into this, and things started to change and take on a different momentum.

Deeper Into the Inner Self

I reached out to my TM teacher, Mina. We planned to meet so she could show me some advanced techniques to help get me through this. As I walked into the building where I had learned to practice TM years before, I felt safe, as if it was a homecoming. We sat in a room, and I cried, the tears flowing down my face and onto my jacket, soaking the front of it. She looked at me with her kind eyes, looking deeper into my soul, and that gave me comfort. We sat that way for a while. She gave me the time I needed, and I was grateful for that.

Together, she showed me some things I could add to my practice throughout the day that would help me.

I took it all in, feeling that it was helping me already. At the end of our meeting, she went into the other room and came back holding a single long-stemmed red rose and a book. It was a gift for me. The book was from Bob Roth, and the quote on the back was from Ray Dalio about how TM was so important in his life. I smiled, feeling reassured as the reason I had even learned to practice years ago was because of Ray Dalio.

I went back to New York that weekend with my husband to see Apollonia, who I continued to see throughout this ten-week journey. So many beautiful things started to happen. Upon the suggestion from Christen, we went to a monastery in Astoria, New York, on our way home to Boston that Sunday. This was a deeply beautiful experience. I felt so grateful to have the opportunity to go and pray there. I fell to my knees, and a calm came over me as I released tears.

The following week, I read *Super Attractor,* the new book from Gabby Bernstein. I took my notebook and my phone (I was listening to the audiobook) and went to sit in Boston's famous Public Garden. It was a beautiful, crisp, sunny fall day. The leaves had just started to change colors and fall, and I sat, facing the sun, on a bench close to the little duckling statues. I had so many fond memories of taking my daughters to the statues when they were toddlers. I would sit on the very same bench and watch them climb the little iconic statues. On this day, that gave me great comfort.

As I sat facing the sun listening to Gabby's book, that particular chapter was saying that I could ask for a sign to know if I was on the right path. Since I had decided the last week that I was going to do a double mastectomy with reconstruction, I hadn't spoken to my surgeon yet. So I asked for a sign to make sure that this was the right decision for me. I was clear about my question and asked that if this was the right path for me, I would receive roses within the next day. No one had sent me roses in years, so I thought this would be a very clear sign.

As I walked through the Boston Common back toward my apartment building, it was the first time in the past six weeks that I didn't feel complete despair. Maybe it was because I had gone to do something that was simple and had brought me great joy in the past. Sitting on that bench, listening to an author that I trusted. I was grateful for those simple things.

When I entered the lobby of my building and greeted all of the wonderful staff that had become family over the years, I saw a small beautiful bouquet of white roses. It's very typical to see gorgeous flower deliveries, especially at that time of day. I smiled and said, "How pretty. Someone will be really happy to receive these," as they were being put on a delivery cart along with packages for the porter to distribute. The staff smiled and told me that the pretty flowers were for me and they had just arrived about an hour ago. How incredible was this? This was the clear sign that I had asked for only an hour ago. I looked at the card, and it was from an old friend I hadn't seen in years. I was so overwhelmed with how this had just worked—just like that.

That's when my journey started to have a shift in momentum. It was a few days later on a Sunday that the woman at church mentioned I should go see Dr. Ellis, a Naturopath and MD who has helped so many like me, and that he perhaps could help me. It was a miracle that I was able to get in to see him the following Saturday because he had a three-month waiting list. That Monday, October 21st, I could feel the shift, things starting to fall into place without much effort from me. Up until then, I was trying really hard. Now that I knew what I wanted and was comfortable with my decision, and maybe because I was more at peace, things started to happen naturally. Apollonia did a remote healing for me that evening, and I drifted off to sleep.

That week was when everything changed for me. A friend sent me a Hay House series that featured speakers talking all about healing. I was so grateful for this because it was perfectly timed. I was ready to hear it. I listened each night to the speakers in each series, taking into my current situation what I could from their teachings. That was an intense week of emotions. Many highs and many lows. I wasn't comfortable with my current medical team, but I just didn't know why. I had appointments that week with doctors that left me feeling so upset. I just wasn't connecting with their approach. I knew in my gut that this is not where I was meant to be.

Navigating Emotions

I lashed out at my family, especially that week. My patience was nonexistent. Although I had made a decision medically, emotionally I was still all over the place.

The littlest thing would set me off. My daughters were trying their hardest, but at moments, I couldn't see it. It's almost like I was trying to detach from them. I fell into old patterns that week, telling everyone that everything was okay, but taking it out on myself and my family. This felt terrible. Worse than it ever had in the past. We were all tired and scared. A big source of my stress was that, deep down, I knew I wasn't with the right medical team for me. I just didn't know what to do about it.

Toward the end of the week, as my appointment with Dr. Ellis was approaching, I was feeling more anxious than ever. I worked myself into a complete mental frenzy. There was still so much good around me, but I just had lost sight of it. It's as if I was temporarily blind. Slowly things started to change. The energy started to shift, a little glimpse here and there. My sister had been in Russia on business and sent me a picture of candles she had lit for me at the Church of the Epiphany in Red Square. I stared at this picture on my phone, and it felt like I could feel the warmth from the flame of the candle. Something came alive inside of me that had been sleeping. That same night, my little godson arrived for his very first visit to America. The trip was planned long before my diagnosis, and I was looking forward to seeing him and decided to go ahead with the visit. I am grateful I did.

The next morning, I went to see Dr. Ellis, and he suggested I get a second opinion. Then everything changed. Right away. I left his office feeling like I was going to be okay for the first time since my diagnosis.

There were a lot of miracles and things that happened to me each day after that.

I had been gifted tickets from Joy to see Gabby Bernstein speak about her new book *Super Attractor* that I had finished reading in the park a few weeks before. I went straight there after my appointment with Dr. Ellis to hear Gabby speak. It was everything I dreamed it would be, and more. The energy had completely changed around me. I felt that every single word that was coming out of her mouth was directed toward me. The questions that came from the audience were as if they were coming out of my mouth. I soaked it all up, remembering that I had gotten a clear sign the week before (a tool from her book) that I was on the right path.

That weekend, I released whatever rage I had left inside of me. I lashed out in frustration at Thalia, and I felt so sick after that that I knew this method was no longer serving me or my family. This pattern of expressing my fear this way and taking it out on the people closest to me was over. It was something I had grown up watching and receiving myself, and it didn't feel good. I had done so much work throughout all my years as a mother to make sure that I would not treat my daughters this way, and now in my darkest moments, this is what naturally came out. I went back to patterns from my own childhood that I had not repeated in raising my children, and now they were front and center. I could feel immediately that this was not meant for me or them. I recognized I had been wrong in my reaction, and that yelling and being hysterical wasn't going to help me and only scare them more.

I didn't want to scare them. I knew how they felt. I understood firsthand what it felt like to be a teenager and have a parent that was sick. My heart broke for them because I could imagine what they were feeling. The last thing I wanted to do was to recreate my childhood for them. Yet by yelling and reacting the way I had, I was doing exactly that. I went to the most familiar place, even though it was a great source of pain for me. I recognized what was happening. I am grateful that I had the awareness and tools to support and adjust, especially for them. I am hopeful that one day they will understand that I love them more than anything and they are the greatest gifts in my life. I try each and every day to make sure they feel loved and safe, but sometimes I make mistakes. I know that I have to learn from this and forgive myself so that we can grow as a family. I asked for help with this that night in my prayers, and the next day, October 28, 2019, my prayers were answered.

A SoulCycle friend had reached out to me about a therapist that worked at Massachusetts General Hospital (MGH) who had helped her with her children when she had breast cancer years ago. I reached out to her, and we had arranged to meet. When I walked into MGH and checked in to my appointment, it felt like home. I could feel the warmth around me. I knew a big part of this was because this is where my father had been for all his medical care throughout his illness. That day was the 30th anniversary of his death. I knew on that day that I needed to be at MGH for my surgery. I didn't know how, but I knew I would be there.

Later that afternoon, I had insisted that my husband remove a tooth that I had had a root canal in a few years ago. This was part of all the research I had done on my own, as well as Apollonia saying she sensed that the left side of my face had something going on. There was this overwhelming statistic that kept popping up over and over again that 98% of all women who have breast cancer also have a root canal on the same side of their bodies. I am not sure how accurate this is, but it got my attention.

Although I had no symptoms and the X-ray showed no issues, I knew in my gut that it had to come out. My husband, a highly skilled and well-respected dentist, obliged me, mostly to keep me happy. We were utterly SHOCKED when after much difficulty to remove the tooth, we found a small cyst was attached to one of the roots. The cyst was almost the same size as the tumor in my breast. I was so happy to have that tooth removed. I am so glad that I trusted my instinct, and so was my husband. This is now something he is aware of with all of his female patients, and we are both so grateful for that.

The next day, I reached out to a friend who is an oncology doctor at MGH. I also reached out to another friend whose neighbor was a radiologist at MGH, and they both came back with the same recommendation of who I should see. This was how I found my incredible surgeon, Michelle.

All the while, I was listening to all of the Hay House healing speakers each night. They were so informative and helpful. I found one in particular talking about exactly what I was missing. Her name is Lynne McTaggart, and she was talking about the power of group prayer and intention. This piqued my interest. Although I had been praying every day—each morning on my own or at this point, various times throughout the day as well—what she was talking about was new to me. I embraced it and quickly reached out to her on social media, asking her for tips on how to set up my own prayer circle. She got back to me right away with a 15-minute YouTube video on how I could do this for myself. I was so grateful; this changed everything for me and continues to be one of the greatest joys in my life even today.

The Power of Prayer

I immediately also downloaded and listened to her book *The Power of 8*. It changed my life. The way it works is that a minimum of eight people come together to pray for the same intention at the same exact time for ten minutes. This works both virtually as well as coming together in the same room at the same time when possible. She had witnessed so many people healing from this type of organized prayer intention that I knew I had to do it. I picked up my phone, and without thinking, started texting friends individually from all different parts of my life and all different religious backgrounds and practices. Within one hour, all ten women had replied that they were available and willing to come to my house the following week, and we would do this together. It was the easiest thing I have ever done in my life. I put the whole group together on one text and sent them the video clip from the author so they knew what to expect.

When we came together the following week, it was like nothing I had ever felt before. I sat on the floor, and they all sat around me, each putting their hands on my body. The room was dark, and only the city lights were streaming in. My intention that night was for all the cancer to be removed during my surgery and for me to heal completely and to go on to live a long, happy life with my husband and daughters. I could feel the vibration of all their energy coming through me during the prayer. It was beautiful. I knew that night that I was going to be healed.

After my prayer, we sat around the table and the women all met each other. It was magical. We prayed that night for three other people who needed our prayers. I am happy to report that all of our prayers were answered that night and continue to be. This group has prayed for me during my surgery and my healing every night, remotely. I could feel their prayers even though we were never in the same room all together after that initial night on November 8th. Since then, other groups have formed as people have heard about how incredible our experience was and remains. Our prayer circle has grown to 16 people now, and we pray at least once a week for whoever needs it. It has been one of the greatest gifts in my life.

Having formed this circle was the single most important thing I did during my healing journey. This is for everyone and works for all. This can be in addition to what you already practice. This is a game changer in every single way.

This brings me to the last ten days before my surgery. So many things had happened that would change me forever. I had a new medical team that I was so comfortable with, I had mended relationships, I had made peace with my past, I had forgiven myself, I had forgiven others. All the work that I had been trying to do my whole adult life I had done in this, the most difficult time in my life. In my darkest moments. I knew in order for my incredible doctors to heal me, I need to do my part. This was a wake-up call for me, plain and simple.

I spent the days and nights leading up to my surgery accepting whatever emotions were coming up. I knew I had done the work. Like a person running a marathon, I had logged my miles, I had trained, and I was ready. There wasn't anything left for me to do but just go run the race. As I type these words, I am crying. I hope they bring you peace and comfort during your difficult time.

The weekend before my surgery, I went out on a date with my husband, just the two of us. I looked across the table, hopeful for our future. As we toasted, I said what a life-changing ten weeks this journey has been. It was so hard, but here I was, ready for my race. I had found the peace I needed to go forward with my life.

The day before my surgery, I received a blessing after church from my wonderful priest. All the parishioners had left. As I knelt in front of the altar to receive my blessing, tears flooded my face. These tears felt different. Like a release. I was grateful for my faith that had carried me through once again.

The next morning before dawn, Joy came to pick me up and take me in for my surgery. My husband and I had decided it would be best if he was there in the morning so the girls wouldn't be alone. As we drove to MGH, I knew this was the right thing for me, but I was still scared. Once I had checked in and saw all of the incredible people who would be helping me heal that day, I had a shift. I felt overwhelmed with gratitude. So, I told them. I took a moment to stop and thank each one for all the sacrifices they made to be there that day to help me. I will never forget their faces—not a single one of them. I could see that their eyes also got teary; I knew I was in the best possible hands. I then told them to make sure to get it all out—I had to get that last part in. The last thing I remember was holding Dr. Michelle's hand and looking into her eyes. I saw her incredible kindness and warmth. She looked like an actual angel as I drifted off to sleep . . . .

REFLECTIONS ON HEALING

Release Your Anger

Saying you accept something is not the same as truly accepting it. You have to release your anger about it first. Listen to the words you use—that's a great way to check and see if you are still holding on to anger about a situation. The word "but" is a great indicator that you haven't let shit go. I am not saying bury your head in the sand and let people and situations walk all over you. I am saying the opposite.

Releasing the anger you feel toward a person or a circumstance and accepting it for what it is gives you freedom. Once you start practicing, it becomes easier and easier. Even the worst situations can be released. Close your eyes and picture the person or the situation the way you wish it was. Then, as hard as it may feel in the moment after you have this visual, send that person or situation a blessing. Yup, bless that. It works. Once you start practicing this, you'll see that it takes the power away from the person or situation and brings it back to you. This is a very liberating feeling.

Go to Places Where You Have Had Good Memories

Happy memories—the energy in those places will spark that same feeling in you today, and you will feel better. Ask for a sign that you are on the right path. Going to sit on the bench that day in the Public Garden alone with my book brought back such fond memories and gave me comfort. Find your "bench" where you have a good, sweet memory and go there if you can, or look at a picture of it to help you if you can't get there. Once you are there, just ask your question. Ask for a sign that you are on the right path.

Be True to Yourself

It's okay for our kids to see that we don't have our shit together all the time. That we are human and vulnerable and need help. Instead of using energy to make everything okay for them during this time, be yourself. My girls are teenagers, but I think every stage has its moments where you can apply this. If your kids are little, keep it simple. If they watch more TV because you just don't feel like playing, it's okay; they'll be fine. If you can't take them to a birthday party because you don't feel like dealing with them, arrange for them to go with someone else. If they miss a sports practice, it won't kill them, I promise. All of the pressure we put on ourselves as mothers is ridiculous. Use this time to break some or all of those patterns. In the big picture, it just doesn't matter. Kids, regardless of age, just want to feel loved. Be kind and compassionate to yourself. They will see this, and through that, they will learn how to love themselves and feel loved.

Just because you have done things a certain way up until now doesn't mean you should continue that way. Look at what you are saying yes to and ask yourself why. Ask yourself what's going to make you feel better today, and do that. Keep it simple, and there is no need to overexplain to anyone why you didn't show up. Even if they ask. Even though they mean well, people will want you to "be yourself" because it's less fearful for them. This is not intentional, but subconscious, it's okay. This is your time, and you need to do only what you truly want to do. If you really don't feel like doing something, don't do it. A test I would use is, "If I don't show up to this, will someone die?" If the answer is no, then you don't need to go!

Heal Your Trauma

I believe holding on to trauma can cause the body to be in dis-ease. You may not even realize this is happening. It could have become completely normal for you to have these memories playing in the back of your mind daily like I did. Then new things pile on, which is exactly what had happened to me. There is no longer space for these things to live within you; you need all your energy to get well.

Identifying them is the first step. This is something that you can do on your own and doesn't require anything but you being honest with yourself. Really think about what you have been holding on to. It doesn't have to be some big event or death, but something in your life that hurt you that you still think about each day. It can also be something that was so traumatic that you try not to think about it because it hurts too much. Well, trying not to think about it is thinking about it.

I was experiencing a combination of these when I got diagnosed. I had my old favorites that I had held onto for years. I had seen therapists, gone to workshops, and done a lot of work around my childhood trauma. I had all the tools. The story that played in my mind on repeat was that I had a difficult childhood, my father died, my family relationships were strained and stressful, my marriage was in big trouble, and I had been recently scammed and lost my startup business along with a ton of money.

The most recent one was the tipping point and the one that put me over the edge. I had come up with an idea for a software program that would connect independent freelance nail technicians with clients who would like to have a nail service at home. The intention of the company was to provide a platform for women to be able to work freelance on their own and to build their own business with very little startup cost. I had the best intentions and put my whole heart and soul into making it a success. I built an inexpensive app overseas to test the concept, and it worked! It started to do well and get some traction. Eventually, the simple app I had built to test the concept no longer worked to meet the needs of this growing business, so I looked for a local company that could build the next version and help us build and scale the business. I found one based in Boston that seemed to do exactly what I needed. I cashed out my retirement account and brought on an investor as well. In the beginning, this was going great. Then as time went on, I started to notice that certain things just didn't seem right. Calls weren't being returned; software builds were delayed. I was worried. The reason this was happening was the company I had hired was really a front for a Ponzi investment scheme. The person responsible is in jail because he had stolen from many people, including me. Not only had I invested my own money, but even worse, I had invested my friend and business partner's money. This made me sick to my stomach.

I felt so violated. This business that I was building to help people had been destroyed. I had invested money, years, and so much love into this. My family had made sacrifices in order for me to do this, and just like that, it was all gone. This was my tipping point.

All of my past trauma came rushing in to meet and welcome the newest member of the club. All of my life's traumas came back one by one. I started in a downward spiral. I was just so sad. My marriage was at an all-time low, and this sent us even further apart. Things I had never dealt with from years ago came flooding back, taking down all the good along the way. Coming to terms with this was hard. I was embarrassed—how could I have made such a wrong decision? I did what I could to minimize the damage. I was able to pivot businesswise, do what I had to do legally to protect myself and the business, and get back on my feet. I was able to find a new technology partner, and we decided to work on something completely new and start over; we were not able to continue work on the original concept. This experience was a huge learning lesson for me. I always followed my gut about everything, and this time I had overlooked the warning signs. This was a sobering reminder to always follow my gut.

Is there something that you are holding on to from your past that you spend time thinking about that doesn't make you feel good? This diagnosis is a clear message to deal with that and let it go, once and for all. No matter how many times you have tried in the past, this is now the time. You simply do not have the space for it anymore, no matter what it is. You will need all of your energy to be focused on your healing. You don't have any time to waste on things that do not help you. I can guarantee you that thinking about past situations where you were hurt absolutely will not help you.

The first step in releasing is to identify what it is. You know what it is and do not have to look to anyone else to tell you or to confirm. The simplest way to see it is to listen to your gut. If you have that uneasy feeling when you think about it, that's it. Once you can identify it, no matter how severe it was, accept that it happened. Next, bless it. Yup, you heard me, bless it. I know this sounds absolutely nuts, but it isn't. What's nuts is thinking about it and being so upset about it and making yourself sick—that's nuts. Then say out loud, "I forgive "this," and it can leave me now." Do this practice every time it creeps up in your mind. These three steps will release you from this heavy burden you have been caring for and make room for your healing.

Steps to Release

- Identify - by paying attention to how you feel when it comes up.
- Accept - that it happened. It helped me to say out loud what had happened.
- Bless - it. This can be the tough one. It feels awkward at first but gets easier and works.
- Forgive - Say out loud, "I forgive it."

Keep it simple. You have enough to worry about now; you don't need to add to your plate. Write it down on an index card and keep it in your wallet. When it creeps up and you are having a tough moment, you can take this out and read it. If you're like me, you will need more than one card; that's okay. This is something that you can do for yourself that will make you feel better in your hardest moments.

Believe me, I understand. I was the queen of, "but how can I let it go it was so real and painful?" You no longer have time for this attitude. Even if you have done everything else like I had and told yourself this was behind you, if it is still coming up in your thoughts and gives you that feeling in your gut, you have more work to do to release it. For the sake of time, because of what you are going through, do this. It worked for me. It's simple and easy and free, and you can do it anywhere. You can add this to whatever you are already doing to help you with past trauma or pain. This can be an added tool that can give you relief. If you have been suppressing and haven't done anything to help yourself heal, this is a great place to start.

Make sure during this time to pay attention to relationships that were feeding the story. For example, if you have gone through a painful divorce and that has become part of how you identify yourself, that's how other people see you too. Make a conscious decision that you no longer want to identify that way. Friends are going to be so used to you bringing it up because that has been a huge part of who you were. Once you make the shift and start putting this into practice, you will naturally not want to bring it up as much. If friends bring it up, tell them clearly that you are working on releasing that trauma and talking about it and reliving it is not helping you during this time of healing. Your friends can help you stay on track.

I know firsthand that trauma is real and how hard it is to leave it in the past. This is something I struggled with my entire life. When I got diagnosed, I also knew that there was no more space for these traumas in my mind and body. I had no other choice but to let them go. This felt uncomfortable because these had become such a big part of who I was. I had become so comfortable in these stories that at first, it was hard to leave them. But I did it, and you can do it too. Just take the first step. Use this simple technique and start with one. Once you start to feel better, if you have more to do, move on to the next one. You will feel lighter, and this will create the space that you need, especially now more than ever.

Also, you don't need to get a cancer diagnosis to start this practice. This is for anyone who has been through tough times, which is everyone.

You need to free yourself in order to get better. This will help you.

Chapter seven:
The Next Chapter

I opened my eyes and looked around. I was in a hospital recovery room and had an oxygen mask on. First thought was, well, this is good. I am alive; second thought was I really need to pee. The nurses came right in, smiling, and my sister was just a minute behind them. I looked at her, and I could tell by her eyes that I was okay. I asked her if the doctors had been able to put in implants and her reply was, "Yes, and they look amazing." It was so sweet and comforting. Most importantly, the surgery was a success, and I was free of cancer. The rest of the day at the hospital was a blur. I know that my family and friends were all there throughout the day, and I remember my incredible surgeon, Michelle, coming by to see me before she was going home. She was wearing a SoulCycle sweatshirt, which made me smile. I told her that one day I looked forward to riding with her side-by-side in Soul Cycle class. This woman, and the incredible Dr. Eric—an angel plastic surgeon, along with many others, had cut the cancer out of me and given me a second chance at life. What a gift.

Once everyone had left, it was my sister who stayed with me. She held my hair back when I threw up because of the effects of the anesthesia; she made sure I had everything I needed: a yummy gluten-free pasta dish from one of my favorite restaurants, Starbucks tea, and the original *90210*, Season One. She stayed right next to me until I fell asleep that night, and when I woke up the next day, she was right back sitting next to me. All the years we had been apart evaporated. Her loving actions were better than any words. She had shown up for me when I needed her most, without me asking. That's love.

I continued to heal really well and get very good news regarding pathology and future treatment. All I would need going forward was hormone therapy to block my estrogen; this was a huge blessing. There is not a single day that goes by that I don't realize how incredibly lucky I am. However, I am still human, and some days are still so hard. I thought once the cancer was removed that I would be done with this. I thought that all my ten weeks in "the waiting room" between my diagnosis and my surgery had made me so present that I could put this past me. I was wrong.

Instead, I realized that this was part of my story now; it has changed me completely. It has changed my relationships. It has shown me things as they truly are and have been for a long time. Cancer was my greatest teacher. Don't misunderstand, I am not in any way saying it was "a gift." I am saying it was my life's greatest lesson. The hardest lesson I have ever had to learn. I am still learning.

I learned that it is okay to be exactly who I am. I learned that forgiveness and acceptance are not just things I should say I do, but that I should actually do. I learned to love myself and that I am enough just how God made me. I learned that a mother's love is stronger than I can describe in words. I learned that people are so good, and everyone is trying their best. I learned that kindness is everything. I learned to forgive myself. I learned that everything doesn't have to appear perfect. I learned that my faith in God, once again, carried me through. I learned to surrender and stop fighting. I learned that life is meant to be enjoyed. I learned that the human spirit is so powerful. I learned that prayer makes everything better. I learned that our time here on Earth is limited, and we are all here to help each other. I learned that things I was ashamed of from my past didn't matter. I learned I came from a strong woman. I learned I am a strong woman. I learned that I am loved beyond my wildest dreams.

The things I share are based on what I learned during my experience after my diagnosis. Things I did that helped me, and things I wish I had done but realized after the fact. I still use these tools today on my healing journey, and they bring me great comfort. The reason

I wrote this was to help and connect people. My hope is that it will help you in some way.

Reflections on Healing

Moving Beyond Fear

I always had chosen fear. I think this happened after I lost my father. I had lived with this fear around my health. I had lived with this as an underlying theme of my life. Start to think of these old thought patterns as an abusive relationship. Something you know is wrong and hurting you, but you just can't leave. This had escalated to a point where if I stayed any longer, it would have killed me. Fighting to survive each day is no way to live. I woke up one morning and realized that the reason I couldn't love myself or receive love from others is that I was in an abusive relationship with fear. It's as if a light switch was turned on, and I suddenly saw it for what it really was. I had lived 30 years with one constant thought that was the basis of everything: that one day, what happened to my dad would probably happen to me. This was the truth. I wonder if other children who have lost their parents struggle with this.

This could also happen if you witnessed or helped a parent through an illness. The fear of the same thing happening to you could be lingering in the back of your mind. These thoughts could turn into fears, and this same type of "relationship" could be happening. Watching a parent in a vulnerable position like that is hard. Each time you fill out your medical history, it is there for you to read in your own words as a nice reminder.

There is no closer "it could happen to me" relationship than your parents with whom you share so much genetically. Yet I believe the additional stress of worrying about it will, most likely, bring you something unwanted. It's so hard to break this conditioning, but it is vital, especially if you are reading this and have just received a diagnosis. It might even make you want to go deeper into that "relationship" with fear because you are so comfortable there. This will exhaust you and create so much more stress and anxiety. Believe me, I know firsthand having just gone through it.

Change Your Mind Frame

Changing the frame in which you see this experience is an absolute necessity in order for you to move forward with a new healthy story of your own. Here are the steps for you to "break up" with fear and create a new health story all your own.

Force yourself to be grateful, even if you have to fake it in the beginning. I can't think of a better time to fake it till you make it. I know it's really hard now to find something to be grateful for when you are in the middle of this shitstorm, but here is a simple way to do this that is easy and simple:

Keep a notebook and pen by your bedside. Each day from now on, when you wake up, sit up in your bed before you do anything else and write something you are grateful for. Write the date and fill in the blank: "I am grateful for_____." It has to be at least one thing. If you can't find anything that day, write, I am grateful that I woke up today. Some days that will be it. That's okay.

This gratitude ritual is free, easy, and available to you right away. This simple change to the start of each day will begin to change your relationship with fear. Anyone can do this; it can be added to your already-existing gratitude practice, or this can be your only gratitude practice. It works for everyone in any situation. This will give you something else to think about first thing in the morning other than the fear-based thinking you are used to. Even for that one minute, it will start to reframe your story.

The reason I recommend doing this in a notebook is because when you have dark moments or days, it will be easily available for you to go back to and read through. I often go back to read what I was grateful for, and seeing it in my own writing is powerful. And since you've dated each entry, it will be even more powerful because you'll see that on especially hard days, you were able to get through them, and the very next day, you still found something to be grateful for. This will be one of the greatest gifts that you give yourself.

Some mornings you will fill many lines with things you are grateful for, and some mornings you will feel like a fraud writing something down, but do it no matter what. Do it anyway. Just do it. Take it with you everywhere. Don't miss a day. Even if you forget in the morning, just fill it in when you remember. Keep it simple for yourself.

Once you start this practice, it will soon become second nature. It will make you feel good, even for a few moments each day. This will start to change the way in which you frame your health story. Giving gratitude the starting lineup in your day and making fear wait to make an appearance will start to diminish its power and hold over you. This can be a slow, gradual release, or it can be an "aha!" moment when you realize that fear is not the first thing you think about. This will give energy to better things in your life and make you feel better.

The key is to recognize that the health journey and life of your parents is not your life. You have a different story. Shifting your thinking first thing each day to gratitude will force you to see things differently. Be aware of who you are listening to and what they are saying. Family members who tell you that you're just like your dad was, or you're just like your mom. This could be a trigger, although it is probably very well-meaning if your parent was ill or died or both, but this is not helpful for you to hear right now. Limit these conversations, or just don't have them until you have reframed your thinking around this. We are all individuals on our very own journey.

Start A New Relationship with Your Health

- Each morning, start your day writing in a notebook about what you are grateful for. Make sure you date each entry and write something each day, no matter what.

- Limit your exposure to any old stories about your parents' illness or death that people connect with you.
- Think of your parent who has passed away in a positive light by making a playlist of happy songs that remind you of them, and when you are feeling vulnerable, listen.
- Write a letter to your parent who passed away, forgiving them for leaving you.
- Write a letter to your parent who was ill, forgiving them for any pain that caused you. (You don't give them that letter, it's just for you to release whatever you are holding on to.)

When you start to go down the rabbit hole of despair, find comfort in reading what you are grateful for, as well as the letters of forgiveness you have written. Your own words will bring you more comfort than anything else you could ever read at this time. It will also empower you to break up with this toxic relationship. This will fade away into the background of your life and disappear, allowing you to have your own new story.

This can work for you too. Break up with fear about your health. It doesn't matter how long you have been with fear; you can break up with it and start a whole new story. I remind myself very often that all the times I was scared never changed how anything turned out. It is time now to leave your fear behind you and focus on you.

About the Author

Joanna Chanis is a mother and entrepreneur. She is a Greek American born in Worcester, Massachusetts, who moved to Boston for college 30 years ago and has lived there ever since. Joanna loves to travel, especially to Greece, where she spends time each year with her family and friends. She has owned and operated a restaurant as well as founded a technology start-up. She loves to cook Greek food and share meals with friends. Fashion has always been a huge interest of hers, shoes and handbags especially. Throughout her life, she always felt a deep connection to people and values her relationships more than anything else. She serves as a mentor to young entrepreneurs and also helps teenagers who have lost a parent. When she was diagnosed with breast cancer in 2019, everything changed for her, and she knew that her purpose was clear: to help and connect people. She put her experience and advice together in these pages to do exactly that.

To connect with Joanna, follow her on Instagram: @thewaitingroombook

Made in the USA
Middletown, DE
15 October 2020